# SOFTWARE PROGRAMMING BASICS

AI-GENERATED STEP-BY-STEP GUIDE TO HELP YOU START YOUR SOFTWARE PROGRAMMING JOURNEY WITH EASE

VINAY GOEL

CO-EDITOR: RICHA GOEL

notionpress
.com

INDIA • SINGAPORE • MALAYSIA

ISBN

Hardcase 979-8-89498-828-3
Paperback 979-8-89475-306-5

# Contents

*Preface* ... 9
*Why Should I Learn Programming?* ... 11
*Introduction* ... 13

**Section 1**
**Introduction to Programming**

Ch 01 What is a Programming Language ... 17
Ch 02 Introduction to Java ... 20
Ch 03 Java Syntax ... 22

**Section 2**
**Learn to Code**

Ch 04 Java Variables and Data Types ... 29
Ch 05 Operators ... 32
Ch 06 Control Flow ... 36
Ch 07 Methods, Functions, and Libraries ... 42
Ch 08 How to Read User Input ... 45

**Section 3**
**Let's Code**

Ch 09 Online Coding Platforms ... 51
Ch 10 A Simple Program to Express Your Love for Coding ... 53

Ch 11 Program to Create a Personalized Statement ........ 56

Ch 12 Perform Arithmetic Operations ........ 58

Ch 13 Calculating the Average ........ 61

Ch 14 Finding the Last Digit of a Number ........ 63

## Section 4
## Problem Solving Using if Else

Ch 15 Finding the Largest Number ........ 69

Ch 16 Checking Divisibility By 3 ........ 72

Ch 17 Ternary Operator ........ 74

Ch 18 Determining Odd or Even ........ 76

## Section 5
## Problem Solving Using Multiple if Statements

Ch 19 Largest Among Three Numbers ........ 83

Ch 20 Finding Percentage and Grade ........ 85

Ch 21 Calculating Water Bill ........ 88

Ch 22 Calculate Days in a Given Month ........ 91

Ch 23 Solving the Leap Year Problem ........ 95

## Section 6
## Iterations

Ch 24 Increment and Decrement Operators ........ 103

Ch 25 While Loop ........ 105

Ch 26 DO-While Loop ........ 108

Ch 27 For Loop ... 111

Ch 28 Break and Continue Statements ... 114

**Section 7**
**Problem Solving Using Loops**

Ch 29 Find the Nth Power of 2 ... 123

Ch 30 Find GCD By Iteration ... 126

Ch 31 Prime Number Checker ... 130

Ch 32 Finding Prime Numbers From 1 to N Using Iterations ... 133

**Section 8**
**Code Locally on Your Machine**

Ch 33 How to Compile and Run a Java Program Locally ... 141

Ch 34 Essential Java Development Tools ... 144

Ch 35 IntelliJ IDEA ... 148

**Section 9**
**Progressions**

Ch 36 Arithmetic Progression ... 155

Ch 37 Nth Term in an Arithmetic Progression ... 158

Ch 38 Sum of Terms in an Arithmetic Progression ... 161

Ch 39 Geometric Progression ... 164

Ch 40 Nth Term in a Geometric Progression ... 167

Ch 41 Sum of Terms in a Geometric Progression ... 169

## Section 10
## Math Problems

Ch 42 Area of a Circle ........ 179

Ch 43 Finding GCD Using Euclid's Algo ........ 181

Ch 44 Functions in Java ........ 184

Ch 45 Number Systems ........ 187

Ch 46 Converting Decimal to Binary ........ 190

Ch 47 Converting Binary to Decimal ........ 192

Ch 48 Understanding the Modulo Operator ........ 195

## Section 11
## Pattern Printing

Ch 49 How to Solve Pattern Problems ........ 205

Ch 50 Printing Left Half Pyramid of Stars ........ 208

Ch 51 Printing Full Pyramid of Stars ........ 211

Ch 52 Printing Inverted Right Half Pyramid of Stars ........ 214

## Section 12
## Pattern Printing Contd

Ch 53 Printing an Hourglass Pattern of Stars ........ 223

Ch 54 Printing a Hollow Square Pattern of Stars ........ 227

Ch 55 Printing a Hollow Full Pyramid Pattern of Stars ........ 230

Ch 56 Printing a Hollow Diamond Pattern of Stars ........ 233

Ch 57 Floyd's Triangle Pattern ........ 237

## Section 13
## Understanding Java Architecture

Ch 58 Java Architecture ........ 247

Ch 59 Java Development Kit (JDK) ........ 251

Ch 60 Java Runtime Environment ........ 254

Ch 61 Java Virtual Machine (JVM) ........ 257

Ch 62 Java Class Libraries ........ 261

Ch 63 Java Application Programming Interfaces ........ 264

Ch 64 Memory Management ........ 266

## Section 14
## Miscellaneous

Ch 65 Object Oriented Programming ........ 275

Ch 66 C++ Architecture ........ 281

Ch 67 Exploring Java Frameworks ........ 285

Ch 68 Bitwise Operators: AND, OR, XOR, and NOT ........ 288

Ch 69 Commutative and Associative Properties of Bitwise Operators ........ 292

Ch 70 Finding Odd and Even Numbers Using Bitwise AND (&) ........ 297

## Section 15
## Data Structures

Ch 71 Stack vs. Heap Memory ........ 307

Ch 72 Data Structures ........ 311

# Preface

This book is created with the intent of explaining software engineering concepts with short lessons. The world of software programming is overwhelming. Embarking on a journey into software programming is both exciting and challenging. One cannot become a software programmer overnight. You need years of hard work and practice to become a proficient software programmer. But the more difficult task is figuring out where to start. The first step is the most difficult step. While it may seem daunting at first, taking the right steps can make the process manageable and rewarding. There are lot of things you have to go through in your software programming journey, like star patterns, C++, Java, python, JavaScript, react, data structures, OOP, variables, functions, loops, algorithms, time and space complexities, architectures, memory management and lot more. But to understand them, the person should have clear understanding of the basics. This guide aims to provide you with a roadmap for starting your programming journey and building a strong foundation. This guide will build up your base and create connecting strings that will stitch the disconnected dots together and help you visualize the big picture. Once you have gone through this guide, you will be able to connect better to other software programming concepts and will be comfortable in understanding any programming language. Once you grasp the fundamentals, you can explore any language like Java, C++, or others based on your interests and goals. Every programmer started as a beginner, and continuous learning is key to becoming a proficient software developer. Good luck on your programming journey!

# Why Should I Learn Programming?

Learning software programming can be beneficial for many reasons

Software programming is in high demand across various industries. By learning programming skills, you open doors to a wide range of career opportunities, from software development and web development to data science, artificial intelligence, and cybersecurity.

Programming teaches you how to break down complex problems into smaller, manageable tasks and find logical solutions. This analytical thinking and problem-solving approach can be applied to various aspects of life, not just programming.

Programming allows you to bring your ideas to life. You can create software applications, games, websites, and innovative solutions that can make a positive impact on people's lives or businesses.

Software developers are among the highest-paid professionals globally. With experience and expertise, you can command competitive salaries and enjoy financial stability.

Programming allows you to automate repetitive tasks, streamline processes, and increase efficiency in various domains, from business operations to scientific research.

Learning programming can boost your confidence, improve your cognitive abilities, and enhance your ability to learn new skills. It's a rewarding and fulfilling journey that can lead to personal growth and self-improvement.

As technology continues to advance, the demand for skilled programmers is continually increasing. Learning programming now prepares you for future career opportunities and ensures that you stay competitive in the job market.

Overall, learning software programming not only opens up exciting career prospects but also hones your problem-solving abilities, sparks creativity, and empowers you to make a meaningful impact in the digital world.

# Introduction

The only requirement to learn programming is the ability to think logically. Logical thinking is the backbone of programming. It's the process of breaking down a problem into smaller, manageable parts and systematically solving them using logical steps. Whether you're a beginner or already have some coding experience, mastering logical thinking will greatly enhance your programming skills. Logical thinking enables you to approach complex problems in a structured manner, making it easier to identify solutions and create efficient code.

How to approach logical thinking in programming?

**Step 1: Defining the problem**

The first step is to clearly define the problem you want to solve. Take the time to understand what you need your program to achieve and what input it will take. This will help you set a clear goal and direction for your coding process.

**Step 2: Breaking it down**

Next, break down the problem into smaller parts or subproblems. By dividing a complex problem into manageable components, you'll find it easier to understand and solve each piece individually.

**Step 3: Analysing and designing**

Once you've broken down the problem, it's time to analyse and design a solution. This involves thinking about the logic and algorithms required to solve each subproblem efficiently. You can use flowcharts or pseudocode to plan out your program's structure and logic.

### Step 4: Implementing the solution

With a well-designed plan in place, it's time to start coding! Implement your solution by writing the necessary code, following the logical steps and using the programming language of your choice.

### Step 5: Testing and debugging

Testing is a crucial step in the logical thinking process. It helps you identify any errors or bugs in your code. By thoroughly testing your program and fixing any issues that arise, you ensure that it functions correctly and delivers the expected results.

Section 1

# Introduction to Programming

# What is a Programming Language

A programming language is a formal set of rules and instructions that enables humans to communicate with computers. It serves as a medium to write programs that tell computers what to do.

Now, let's understand the elements of a programming language.

### Syntax

Every programming language has its own syntax, which is like a grammar or set of rules that defines how the code should be written. Syntax includes keywords, punctuation, and specific structures that must be followed for the code to be valid.

### Variables and Data

Programming languages allow you to work with different types of data, such as numbers, text, and more. Variables are used to store and manipulate this data during program execution.

### Control Flow

Control flow statements, such as if-else, loops, and switch statements, give you the power to control the flow of execution in your program. These statements enable you to make decisions, repeat actions, and create complex logic.

## Functions and Libraries

Functions are blocks of reusable code that perform specific tasks. They help break down complex programs into smaller, manageable parts. Additionally, programming languages provide libraries—collections of pre-written code—that simplify common tasks and enhance functionality.

Programming languages come in various forms, each with its own purpose and area of application.

## High-level Programming Languages

High-level languages, like Python, Java, and C++, are designed to be closer to human language, making them more readable and easier to understand. They provide abstraction from the machine's low-level details.

## Low-level Programming Languages

Low-level languages, such as Assembly and machine code, are closer to the machine's native instructions. They offer more control over hardware resources but are less user-friendly and more challenging to write and understand.

## Scripting Languages

Scripting languages, like JavaScript and Ruby, are typically used for automating tasks, creating web applications, and enhancing the functionality of existing software.

Programming languages are the backbone of software development. They bridge the gap between human understanding and the complex workings of computers. Learning a programming language opens up a world of possibilities and empowers you to bring your ideas to life through code.

High level programming languages are the ones that are mainly used by software Engineers around the world to develop a program and will be our focus area. If you can code in one language, you can code in any language with very little training because the underlying principles remain same. Most commonly used Programming Languages are Java, C++, Python and C#. You can choose to code in any one of them or any other High Level programming language you are aware of. You can do your own research to decide in which language you want to code. Each one has its own pros and cons. We will be using Java as the base for explaining the concepts but the same concepts can be implemented in other languages as well.

Ch 02

# Introduction to Java

Java is a versatile and powerful programming language used in a wide range of applications, from mobile app development to enterprise software. It is known for its simplicity, readability, and platform independence.

## Benefits of Java

### Platform independence

Java is platform-independent, which means you can write your code once and run it on different platforms without making significant changes. This feature has made Java the backbone of many cross-platform applications.

### Object-Oriented Programming (OOP)

Java follows the object-oriented programming (OOP) paradigm, which allows you to create modular, reusable, and maintainable code. With OOP, you can easily organize and manage complex projects.

### Vast ecosystem and community

Java boasts a vast ecosystem of libraries, frameworks, and tools that make development faster and more efficient. Moreover, the Java community is incredibly active, offering plenty of support and resources for beginners and experienced programmers alike.

# Building Blocks of Java

## Variables and Data Types

Variables allow you to store and manipulate data in your programs. In Java, you need to declare variables and specify their data types, such as int, float, string, or boolean.

## Control Flow

Control flow statements, such as if-else, for loops, and while loops, enable you to control the execution order of your program's statements. These statements help you make decisions and repeat actions based on certain conditions.

## Methods

Methods are reusable blocks of code that perform specific tasks. They allow you to break down your program into smaller, manageable pieces and make your code more organized and modular.

Ch 03

# Java Syntax

Java is known for its clean and structured syntax, making it a great language for beginners and professionals alike.

> **Let's explore the key elements that define the syntax of Java.**

## Package Declaration

Every Java program begins with a package declaration that identifies the location of the file within the directory structure. It helps organize and categorize the code.

## Import Statements

Import statements are used to bring external libraries or classes into our program. They provide access to pre-built functionality, saving us from reinventing the wheel.

## Class Declaration

In Java, everything revolves around classes. A class is a blueprint or template that defines the structure and behaviour of objects. It acts as a container for our code.

## Main Method

The main method serves as the entry point of a Java program. It's where the execution begins. Every Java application must have a main method.

## Statements and Blocks

Java programs consist of statements, which are individual instructions that perform specific actions. Statements are organized into blocks, denoted by curly braces, { }.

## Variables and Data Types

Variables store data within our programs. Java is a statically-typed language, meaning variables must have a declared data type. Common data types include int, float, boolean, and string.

## Operators

Operators are used to perform operations on data, such as mathematical calculations or logical comparisons. Java provides a variety of operators, including arithmetic, assignment, comparison, and logical operators.

A typical program consists most of these elements but you may or may not need all elements in a program. Here's a simple program that displays "Hello, World!" on the screen:

```
package package1;
public class HelloWorld {
    public static void main(String[] args) {
        System.out.println("Hello, World!");
    }
}
```

In this code, we have a class named "*HelloWorld*" that contains the main method. Inside the main method, we use the "System.out.println" statement to print the message "Hello, World!" to the console.

## Revision

**How do we approach to solve a problem**

Defining the problem

Breaking it down

Analysing and designing

Implementing the solution

Testing and debugging

**Element of Programming**

Syntax

Variables and Data

Control Flow

Functions and Libraries

**Programming Languages Forms**

High-level Programming Languages

Low-level Programming Languages

Scripting Languages

**Benefits of Java**

Platform independence

Object-Oriented Programming (OOP)

Vast ecosystem and community

**Building Blocks of Java**

Variables and Data Types

Control Flow

Methods

**Elements Of Syntax of Java**

Package Declaration

Import Statements

Class Declaration

Main Method

Statements and Blocks

Variables and Data Types

Operators

## Section 2

# Learn to Code

Ch 04

# Java Variables and Data Types

## Variables

Variables are like containers that hold data within our programs. They allow us to store and manipulate values. In Java, variables have a specific data type, which defines the kind of data they can hold and the operations we can perform on them.

### Declaring Variables

To declare a variable in Java, we need to specify its data type followed by the variable name. For example, we can declare an integer variable called "age" like this: "int age;". This tells Java that we want to create a variable named "age" that can store integer values.

### Primitive Data Types

Java provides several primitive data types, which are the most basic building blocks for variables. Some common primitive data types include int, double, boolean, and char. These data types have a fixed size and represent fundamental values.

### Assigning Values to Variables

Once we've declared a variable, we can assign a value to it using the assignment operator (=). For example, we can assign a value of 25 to our "age" variable like this: "age = 25;".

## Initializing Variables

It's also possible to declare and assign a value to a variable in a single step. This is called initialization. For example, we can initialize our "age" variable with a value of 25 when declaring it: "int age = 25;".

## Variable Naming Conventions

When naming variables, it's important to follow certain naming conventions. Variable names should be descriptive and meaningful, starting with a letter or underscore, and can contain letters, numbers, and underscores. It's also good practice to use camel case for multi-word variable names.

# Common data types in Java

## int

The int data type represents whole numbers(integers) and has a range from -2,147,483,648 to 2,147,483,647. It's commonly used for variables that store age, quantities, and indices.

## double

The double data type represents floating-point numbers with decimal places. It's used for variables that store values with fractional parts, such as height, weight, or measurements.

## boolean

The boolean data type represents a logical value that can be either true or false. It's used for variables that store conditions or control the flow of our programs.

## char

The char data type represents a single character and is enclosed in single quotes. It's used for variables that store individual characters, such as letters, digits, or symbols.

Choosing the right data type is crucial for efficient memory usage and accurate representation of your data.

# Operators

Operators allow us to perform various operations on data, manipulate values, and make our programs more dynamic.

Operators are symbols or special keywords that perform operations on one or more operands. Java provides a wide range of operators, including arithmetic, assignment, comparison, logical, and more that allow us to manipulate data, perform calculations, and create dynamic programs.

## Arithmetic operators

Arithmetic operators perform basic mathematical calculations. We have familiar operators like addition, subtraction (-), multiplication (*), and division (/). Additionally, Java offers the modulus operator (%), which gives us the remainder of a division.

The increment operator (++) adds 1 to a variable, effectively incrementing its value.

The decrement operator (--) subtracts 1 from a variable, effectively decrementing its value.

```
int x = 10;
int y = 5;

int sum = x + y;
int difference = x - y;
int product = x * y;
int quotient = x / y;
int remainder = x % y;

System.out.println("Sum: " + sum);
System.out.println("Difference: " + difference);
System.out.println("Product: " + product);
System.out.println("Quotient: " + quotient);
System.out.println("Remainder: " + remainder);
```

## Assignment operators

Assignment operators are used to assign values to variables. The most common one is the equals sign (=). However, Java also provides compound assignment operators like +=, -=, *=, and /=, which combine assignment with an arithmetic operation.

```
int num = 10;

num += 5; // Equivalent to num = num + 5
num -= 3; // Equivalent to num = num - 3
num *= 2; // Equivalent to num = num * 2
num /= 4; // Equivalent to num = num / 4

System.out.println("Updated num: " + num);
```

## Comparison operators

Comparison operators allow us to compare values and determine relationships. We have operators such as equal to (==), not equal to (!=), greater than (>), less than (<), greater than or equal to (>=), and less than or equal to (<=). These operators return a boolean value, either true or false. For example, the equal to operator (==) compares two values for equality and returns true if they're equal.

```
int a = 10;
int b = 5;

boolean isEqual = a == b;
boolean isNotEqual = a != b;
boolean isGreater = a > b;
boolean isLess = a < b;
boolean isGreaterOrEqual = a >= b;
boolean isLessOrEqual = a <= b;

System.out.println("isEqual: " + isEqual);
System.out.println("isNotEqual: " + isNotEqual);
System.out.println("isGreater: " + isGreater);
System.out.println("isLess: " + isLess);
System.out.println("isGreaterOrEqual: " + isGreaterOrEqual);
System.out.println("isLessOrEqual: " + isLessOrEqual);
```

## Logical operators

Logical operators are used to combine multiple conditions and make decisions based on the results. We have three logical operators: AND (&&), OR (||), and NOT (!). They help us create complex conditions and control the flow of our programs.

- The AND operator (&&) returns true if both conditions it connects are true.
- The OR operator (||) returns true if either of the condition it connects is true.
- The NOT operator returns true if the condition it connects is false.

```
boolean condition1 = true;
boolean condition2 = false;

boolean result1 = condition1 && condition2;
boolean result2 = condition1 || condition2;
boolean result3 = !condition1;

System.out.println("result1: " + result1);
System.out.println("result2: " + result2);
System.out.println("result3: " + result3);
```

## Bitwise operators

Bitwise operators work at the bit level, manipulating individual bits in binary numbers. They are used in low-level programming and operations involving binary data. Some bitwise operators include AND (&), OR (|), XOR (^), left shift (<<), and right shift (>>).

```
int x = 5;
int y = 3;

int bitwiseAnd = x & y;
int bitwiseOr = x | y;
int bitwiseXor = x ^ y;
int leftShift = x << 1;
int rightShift = x >> 1;

System.out.println("bitwiseAnd: " + bitwiseAnd);
System.out.println("bitwiseOr: " + bitwiseOr);
System.out.println("bitwiseXor: " + bitwiseXor);
System.out.println("leftShift: " + leftShift);
System.out.println("rightShift: " + rightShift);
```

# Control Flow

Control flow structures allow us to make decisions, repeat actions, and control the flow of our programs. Java provides several control flow statements, including if-else statements, loops, and switch statements.

## If-Else Statements

The if-else statement is used to make decisions in our programs based on conditions. It allows us to execute a block of code if a condition is true and another block of code if the condition is false.

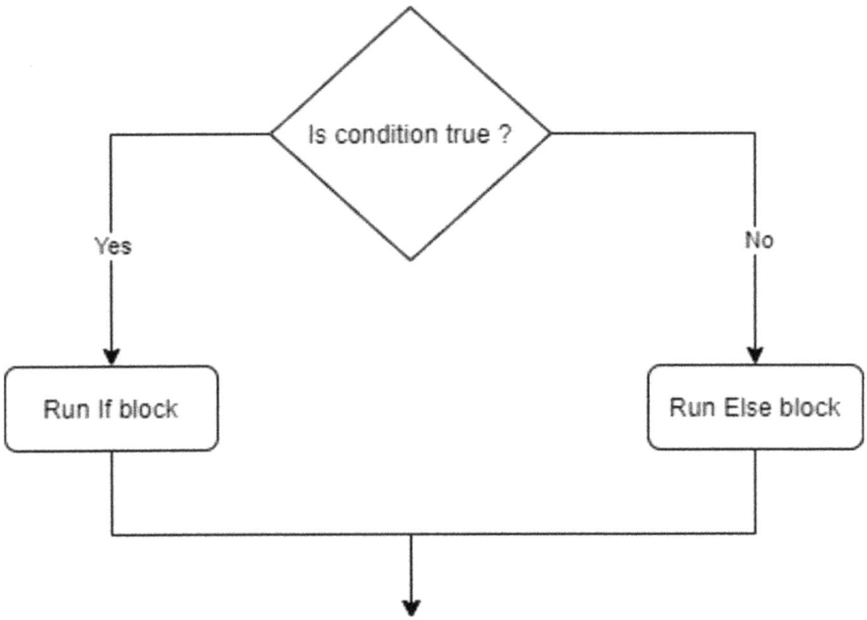

Let's take a look at an example:

```
int age = 18;

if (age >= 18) {
    System.out.println("You are eligible to vote!");
}
else {
    System.out.println("Sorry, you must be 18 or older to vote.");
}
```

## Loops

Loops are used to repeat a block of code multiple times. There are three types of loops: the while loop, the do-while loop, and the for loop.

## While Loop

The while loop repeatedly executes a block of code as long as a condition is true.

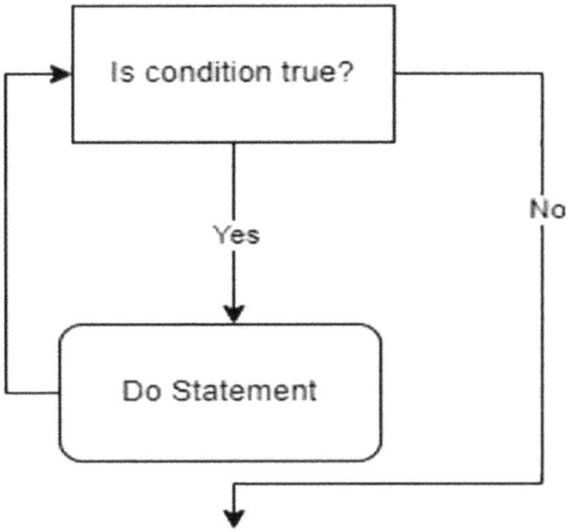

Here's an example:

```
int count = 1;

while (count <= 5)
{
    System.out.println("Count: " + count);
    count++;
}
```

## Do-While Loop

The do-while loop is similar to the while loop, but it executes the block of code at least once before checking the condition.

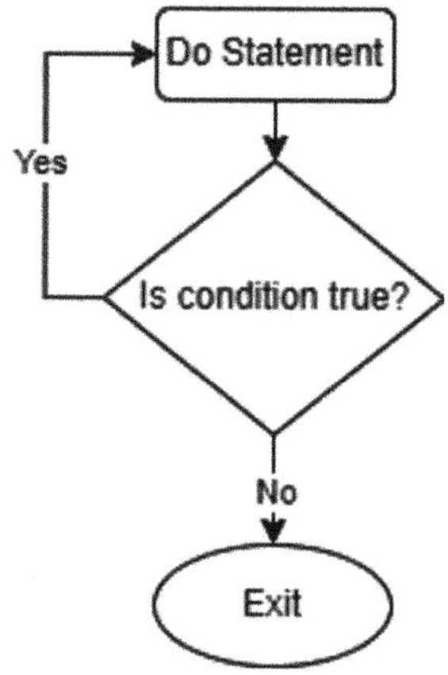


Here's an example:

```
int count = 1;

do {
    System.out.println("Count: " + count);
    count++;
} while (count <= 5);
```

## For Loop

The for loop provides a compact way to iterate over a range of values. It consists of an initialization, a condition, and an increment or decrement.

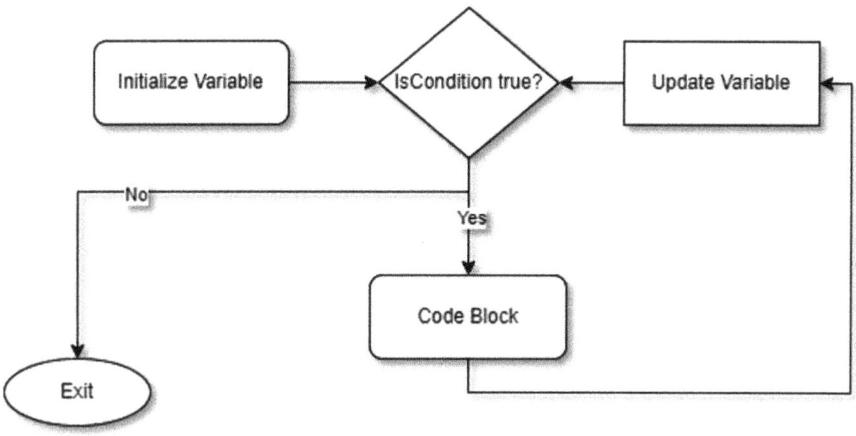


Here's an example:

```
for (int i = 1; i <= 5; i++) {
    System.out.println("Value of i: " + i);
}
```

## Switch Statements

Switch statements are used to perform different actions based on different values of a variable or an expression. They provide an alternative to long chains of if-else statements.

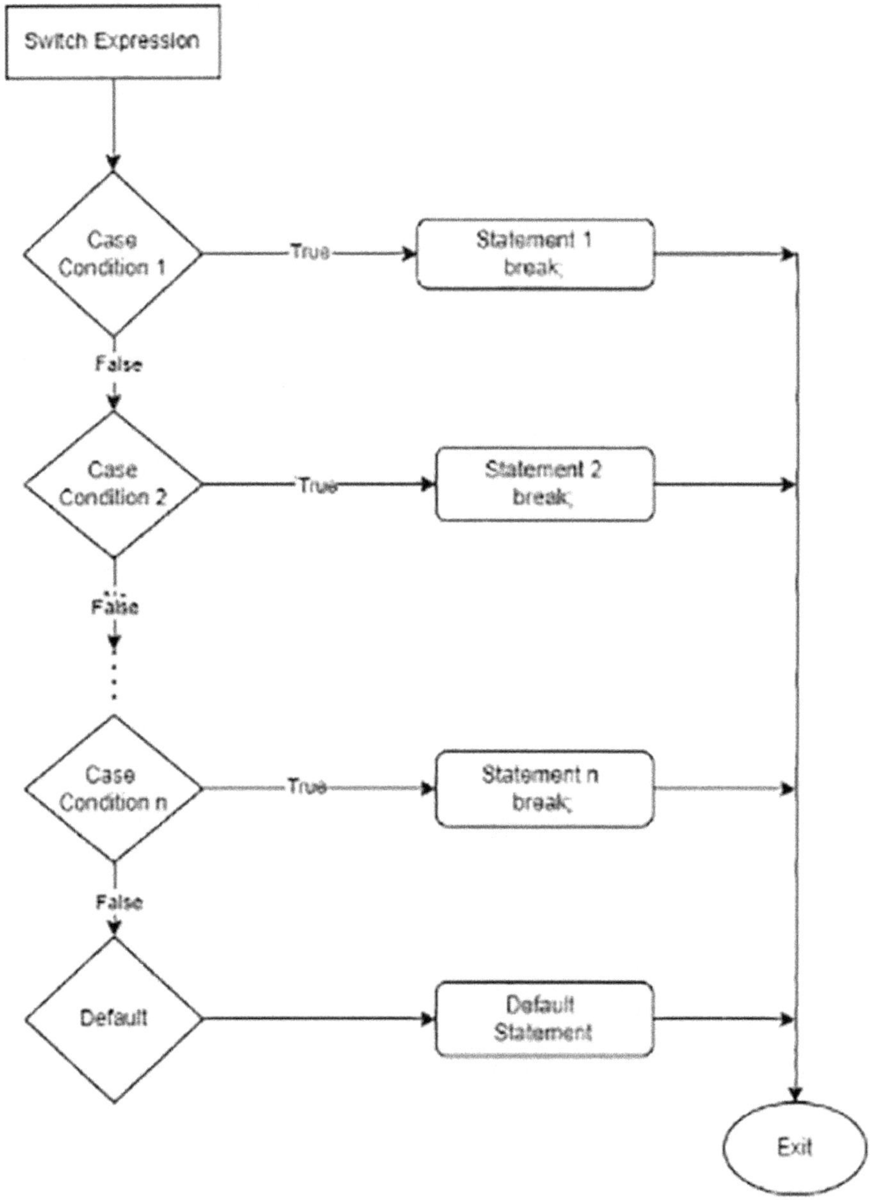
Switch Expression
Case Condition 1
True
Statement 1 break;
False
Case Condition 2
True
Statement 2 break;
False
Case Condition n
True
Statement n break;
False
Default
Default Statement
Exit

Here's an example:

```
int day = 3;
String dayName;

switch (day) {
    case 1:
        dayName = "Monday";
        break;
    case 2:
        dayName = "Tuesday";
        break;
    case 3:
        dayName = "Wednesday";
        break;
    default:
        dayName = "Invalid day";
        break;
}

System.out.println("Today is " + dayName);
```

Ch 07

# Methods, Functions, and Libraries

Methods and functions are essential tools for organizing and reusing code. They allow us to break our programs into smaller, manageable pieces, making our code more readable and maintainable.

## Methods

A method is a block of code that performs a specific task and can be called from other parts of our program. It helps avoid code duplication and promotes modular programming. Here's an example of a method:

```
public static void greetUser(String name) {
    System.out.println("Hello, " + name + "! Welcome to our program.");
}

public static void main(String[] args) {
    String userName = "John";
    greetUser(userName);
}
```

## Functions

Functions are similar to methods but are typically associated with functional programming paradigms. They are self-contained and can return a value. Let's see an example:

```
public static int calculateSum(int a, int b) {
    return a + b;
}

public static void main(String[] args) {
    int num1 = 5;
    int num2 = 3;
    int sum = calculateSum(num1, num2);
    System.out.println("Sum: " + sum);
}
```

## Libraries

Libraries are pre-written code modules that provide a wide range of functionality to developers. They offer ready-to-use methods, classes, and utilities that simplify complex tasks.

Some popular Java libraries include:

java.util: Provides utility classes for data structures, date/time, and input/output operations.

java.io: Offers classes for handling input and output streams.

java.net: Enables network programming and communication.

java.awt and javax.swing: Provide GUI-related classes for building graphical user interfaces.

To use a Java library, we need to import it into our code using the import statement. Once imported, we can leverage the library's classes and methods to enhance our program's functionality. Here's an example:

```
import java.util.Random;

public class RandomNumberGenerator {
    public static void main(String[] args) {
        Random rand = new Random();
        int randomNumber = rand.nextInt(10); // Generates a random number between 0 and 9
        System.out.println("Random Number: " + randomNumber);
    }
}
```

Ch 08

# How to Read User Input

Interacting with users is a common requirement in many applications. The Scanner class is part of the Java standard library and allows us to read input from various sources, including the keyboard. To utilize this class, we need to follow a few simple steps.

## Importing the Scanner Class

First, we need to import the Scanner class into our Java program using the import statement. This enables us to access its functionalities and methods. Here's an example:

```
import java.util.Scanner;
```

## Creating an Instance of Scanner

Next, we create an instance of the Scanner class to start reading user input. We can create the instance by using the new keyword and assigning it to a variable. Here's an example:

```
Scanner scanner = new Scanner(System.in);
```

## Reading Different Data Types

The Scanner class provides various methods to read input of different data types, such as integers, floating-point numbers, and strings. Let's see some examples:

- Reading an integer:

```
System.out.print("Enter an integer: ");
int number = scanner.nextInt();
```

- Reading a floating-point number:

```
System.out.print("Enter a floating-point number: ");
double number = scanner.nextDouble();
```

- Reading a string:

```
System.out.print("Enter a string: ");
String text = scanner.nextLine();
```

**Handling User Input**

When reading user input, it's important to handle potential issues or errors. The Scanner class provides methods like hasNextLine() and hasNextInt() to check if the input matches the expected data type. We can also utilize exception handling to gracefully handle any unexpected input. Here's an example:

```
System.out.print("Enter an integer: ");

if (scanner.hasNextInt()) {
    int number = scanner.nextInt();
    System.out.println("You entered: " + number);
}
else {
    System.out.println("Invalid input. Please enter an integer.");
}
```

By following these steps and utilizing the appropriate methods, you can create interactive programs that respond to user input.

## Revision

**Variables** are like containers that hold data within our programs.

**Primitive Data Types**

- int
- double
- boolean
- char

**Operators** allow us to perform various operations on data, manipulate values, and make our programs more dynamic.

Types of Operators

- Arithmetic operators
- Assignment operators
- Comparison operators
- Logical operators
- Bitwise operators

**Control Flow** allow us to make decisions, repeat actions, and control the flow of our programs.

- If-Else Statements
- Loops
- While Loop
- Do-While Loop
- For Loop
- Switch Statements

**Method** is a block of code that performs a specific task and can be called from other parts of our program. It helps avoid code duplication and promotes modular programming.

**Functions** are similar to methods but are typically associated with functional programming paradigms. They are self-contained and can return a value.

**Libraries** are pre-written code modules that provide a wide range of functionality to developers. They offer ready-to-use methods, classes, and utilities that simplify complex tasks. To use a library, we need to import it into our code using the import/include statement.

**The Scanner class** is part of the Java standard library and allows us to read input from various sources, including the keyboard.

## Section 3

# Let's Code

Ch 09

# Online Coding Platforms

Online coding platforms provide a range of features and resources that facilitate learning and skill development. They offer a platform for coding challenges, online coding contests, practice exercises, and even collaboration with fellow developers. Let's take a closer look at some of the popular platforms out there!

## HackerRank

First up, we have HackerRank. It's a well-known platform that offers a wide range of coding challenges, from basic to advanced levels. You can choose from various programming languages and solve coding problems to enhance your problem-solving skills. HackerRank also hosts coding contests and provides a platform for companies to hire talented developers.

[Link: HackerRank - https://www.hackerrank.com/]

## LeetCode

Next on our list is LeetCode. This platform is widely used by programmers preparing for coding interviews. LeetCode offers a vast collection of coding problems that cover various topics and difficulty levels. It provides detailed explanations and solutions for each problem, making it an excellent resource for interview preparation.

[Link: LeetCode - https://leetcode.com/]

## Codecademy

Codecademy focuses on interactive programming lessons and courses. It provides a hands-on learning experience, allowing you to practice coding directly in your browser. Codecademy offers a variety of programming languages and tracks, including web development, data science, and more. It's an ideal platform for beginners looking to get started with coding.

[Link: Codecademy - https://www.codecademy.com/]

## GitHub

GitHub is not only a version control platform but also a hub for collaborative coding. It allows you to host and showcase your coding projects, collaborate with others, and contribute to open-source projects. GitHub provides a platform to learn from other developers, share your work, and build your coding portfolio.

[Link: GitHub - https://github.com/]

## Codewars

Codewars is a platform that focuses on honing your coding skills through code challenges. It offers a wide range of coding katas, which are small coding exercises that help you practice different concepts and algorithms. Codewars encourages community participation and provides a gamified experience as you progress through higher-ranked katas.

[Link: Codewars - https://www.codewars.com/]

These are just a few of the many online coding platforms available to programmers. Whether you're looking to practice coding, prepare for interviews, learn new concepts, or collaborate with fellow developers, these platforms have got you covered.

# A Simple Program to Express Your Love for Coding

Expressing your passion for coding can be an exciting way to share your enthusiasm. In this article, we will explore a straightforward program that takes input from the user and prints a message that says "<input name> likes coding." By following the steps outlined below, you'll be able to create a personalized message that showcases your love for coding.

## Step 1: Accepting User Input

The first step is to accept input from the user, specifically their name. We will use the Scanner class in Java to accomplish this. The Scanner class allows us to read input from various sources, such as the console.

```
import java.util.Scanner;

public class CodingLikes {
    public static void main(String[] args) {
        Scanner scanner = new Scanner(System.in);

        System.out.print("Enter your name: ");
        String name = scanner.nextLine();

        // More code to come!
    }
}
```

**Step 2: Printing the Message**

Now that we have the user's name stored in the name variable, we can proceed to print the desired message. We will use the System.out.println statement to display the message on the console.

```
System.out.println(name + " likes coding");
```

**Step 3: Completing the Program**

Let's put everything together and complete the program:

```
import java.util.Scanner;

public class CodingLikes {
    public static void main(String[] args) {
        Scanner scanner = new Scanner(System.in);

        System.out.print("Enter your name: ");
        String name = scanner.nextLine();

        System.out.println(name + " likes coding");

        scanner.close();
    }
}
```

**Try running the above code on Leetcode playground.**

- Go to: https://leetcode.com/playground/new/empty
- It will open a coding playground for you. You may need to sign in
- Change the dropdown from C++ to java, since we are coding in java

- Replace the content in Leetcode code section with the above code
- At the bottom left of output section, you will see stdin button. Click on that and write your name in the text area popped up below that. (If you are taking multiple inputs from the user, enter all the inputs, separated by a new line using enter key)
- At top left you will see Run code button. Click on it. your program should give the result in the output window.
- Customize the message with your name, run the program, and see your dedication to coding printed on the screen.

# Program to Create a Personalized Statement

In this chapter we'll explore a simple Java program that allows you to generate a personalized statement that says "<input name> likes <input activity>." By following the steps below, you'll be able to create a unique message that reflects your interests and passions.

## Step 1: Gathering User Input

The first step is to gather input from the user, specifically their name and favourite activity. To achieve this, we will utilize the Scanner class, which allows us to read input from the user through the console.

```
import java.util.Scanner;

public class PersonalStatement {
    public static void main(String[] args) {
        Scanner scanner = new Scanner(System.in);

        System.out.print("Enter your name: ");
        String name = scanner.nextLine();

        System.out.print("Enter your favorite activity: ");
        String activity = scanner.nextLine();

        // More code to come!
    }
}
```

## Step 2: Generating the Personalized Statement

With the user's input captured in the name and activity variables, we can now generate the personalized statement. We'll use the System.out.println statement to display the message on the console.

```
System.out.println(name + " likes " + activity);
```

Let's bring everything together and complete the program:

```
import java.util.Scanner;

public class PersonalStatement {
    public static void main(String[] args) {
        Scanner scanner = new Scanner(System.in);

        System.out.print("Enter your name: ");
        String name = scanner.nextLine();

        System.out.print("Enter your favorite activity: ");
        String activity = scanner.nextLine();

        System.out.println(name + " likes " + activity);

        scanner.close();
    }
}
```

# Perform Arithmetic Operations

In this chapter, we'll explore a simple Java program that takes two numbers as input and prints their sum, difference, division, and multiplication. By following the steps outlined below, you'll be able to create a program that performs these basic arithmetic operations.

## Step 1: Accepting User Input

The first step is to gather input from the user, specifically two numbers. We'll use the Scanner class in Java to achieve this. The Scanner class allows us to read input from various sources, such as the console.

```
import java.util.Scanner;

public class ArithmeticOperations {
    public static void main(String[] args) {
        Scanner scanner = new Scanner(System.in);

        System.out.print("Enter the first number: ");
        double number1 = scanner.nextDouble();

        System.out.print("Enter the second number: ");
        double number2 = scanner.nextDouble();

        // More code to come!
    }
}
```

## Step 2: Performing Arithmetic Operations

Now that we have the two numbers stored in the number1 and number2 variables, we can proceed to perform the desired arithmetic operations.

```
double sum = number1 + number2;
double difference = number1 - number2;
double product = number1 * number2;
double division = number1 / number2;
```

## Step 3: Printing the Results

Finally, we can use the System.out.println statement to display the results of the arithmetic operations.

```
System.out.println("Sum: " + sum);
System.out.println("Difference: " + difference);
System.out.println("Product: " + product);
System.out.println("Division: " + division);
```

Let's put everything together and complete the program:

```java
import java.util.Scanner;

public class AverageCalculator {
    public static void main(String[] args) {
        Scanner scanner = new Scanner(System.in);

        System.out.print("Enter the first number: ");
        double number1 = scanner.nextDouble();

        System.out.print("Enter the second number: ");
        double number2 = scanner.nextDouble();

        System.out.print("Enter the third number: ");
        double number3 = scanner.nextDouble();

        // More code to come!
    }
}
```

# Calculating the Average

In this chapter, we will explore a Java program that solves the problem of finding the average of three numbers.

To calculate the average of numbers, we divide the sum of numbers by the count of numbers.

## Step 1: Accepting User Input

The first step is to gather input from the user, specifically three numbers. We'll utilize the Scanner class in Java to achieve this. The Scanner class allows us to read input from various sources, such as the console.

```
import java.util.Scanner;

public class AverageCalculator {
    public static void main(String[] args) {
        Scanner scanner = new Scanner(System.in);

        System.out.print("Enter the first number: ");
        double number1 = scanner.nextDouble();

        System.out.print("Enter the second number: ");
        double number2 = scanner.nextDouble();

        System.out.print("Enter the third number: ");
        double number3 = scanner.nextDouble();

        // More code to come!
    }
}
```

## Step 2: Calculating the Average

Now that we have the three numbers stored in number1, number2, and number3, we can proceed to calculate their average. To find the average, we sum up the three numbers and divide the sum by 3.

```
double sum = number1 + number2 + number3;
double average = sum / 3;
```

## Step 3: Printing the Result

Finally, we can use the System.out.println statement to display the average to the user.

```
System.out.println("The average of the three numbers is: " + average);
```

Let's put everything together and complete the program:

```
import java.util.Scanner;

public class AverageCalculator {
    public static void main(String[] args) {
        Scanner scanner = new Scanner(System.in);

        System.out.print("Enter the first number: ");
        double number1 = scanner.nextDouble();

        System.out.print("Enter the second number: ");
        double number2 = scanner.nextDouble();

        System.out.print("Enter the third number: ");
        double number3 = scanner.nextDouble();

        double sum = number1 + number2 + number3;
        double average = sum / 3;

        System.out.println("The average of the three numbers is: " + average);

        scanner.close();
    }
}
```

Ch 14

# Finding the Last Digit of a Number

In this chapter, we will discuss the approach, present a step-by-step solution, and provide a code example to solve this problem effectively.

## Understanding the Problem

The problem is to determine the last digit of a given number N. The last digit is the rightmost digit in a number.

## Approach

To find the last digit of a number N, we can follow a simple approach. We will use the modulo operator (%) in Java to calculate the remainder when N is divided by 10. The remainder will be the last digit of the number.

Let's break down the problem into steps:

Step 1: Accepting User Input

First, we need to accept the input value for N. Let's write a simple program to accomplish this:

```
import java.util.Scanner;

public class LastDigitFinder {
    public static void main(String[] args) {
        Scanner scanner = new Scanner(System.in);

        System.out.print("Enter a number: ");
        int N = scanner.nextInt();

        // More code to come!
    }
}
```

## Step 2: Calculating the Last Digit

Once we have the input number N, we can calculate the last digit using the modulo operator.

```
int lastDigit = N % 10;
```

## Step 3: Printing the Result

Finally, we can print the last digit to reveal the outcome. Let's complete the program:

## ➢ Finding the Last Digit of a Number ➣

```java
import java.util.Scanner;

public class LastDigitFinder {
    public static void main(String[] args) {
        Scanner scanner = new Scanner(System.in);

        System.out.print("Enter a number: ");
        int N = scanner.nextInt();

        int lastDigit = N % 10;

        System.out.println("The last digit of " + N + " is: " + lastDigit);

        scanner.close();
    }
}
```

## Revision

**Online Coding Platforms**

- HackerRank - https://www.hackerrank.com/
- LeetCode - https://leetcode.com/
- Codecademy - https://www.codecademy.com/
- GitHub - https://github.com/
- Codewars - https://www.codewars.com/

**How to solve a problem in Leetcode:**

- Go to: https://leetcode.com/playground/new/empty
- It will open a coding playground for you. You may need to sign in
- Change the dropdown from C++ to java, since we are coding in java
- Replace the content in Leetcode code section with your code
- At the bottom left of output section, you will see stdin button. Click on that and write your name in the text area popped up below that. (If you are taking multiple inputs from the user, enter all the inputs, separated by a new line using enter key)
- At top left you will see Run code button. Click on it. your program should give the result in the output window.

Section 4

# Problem Solving Using if Else

Ch 15

# Finding the Largest Number

In the realm of programming, solving problems is at the core of what we do. We will explore a simple yet fundamental problem: finding the largest number among two given numbers, A and B.

## Understanding the Problem

Let's dive into the problem statement. We are given two numbers, A and B, and our task is to determine and print the largest number among the two. To solve this problem, we need to compare the values of A and B and identify the greater one.

## Approach

To find the largest number among two given numbers, we can follow a straightforward approach. We will utilize a conditional statement, such as an "if" statement, to compare the values of A and B. By checking the conditions, we can determine the larger number and print it as the output.

## Step-by-Step Solution

Step 1: Accept the input values for A and B.

```
import java.util.Scanner;

public class LargestNumberFinder {
    public static void main(String[] args) {
        Scanner scanner = new Scanner(System.in);

        System.out.print("Enter the value of A: ");
        int A = scanner.nextInt();

        System.out.print("Enter the value of B: ");
        int B = scanner.nextInt();

        // More code to come!
    }
}
```

Step 2: Compare the values of A and B using an "if" statement.

```
// Step 2: Compare the values of A and B
int largestNumber;
if (A > B) {
  largestNumber = A;
} else {
  largestNumber = B;
}
```

Step 3: If A is greater than B, print A as the largest number. Otherwise, print B as the largest number. Here's the complete program:

```
import java.util.Scanner;

public class LargestNumberFinder {
    public static void main(String[] args) {
        Scanner scanner = new Scanner(System.in);

        System.out.print("Enter the value of A: ");
        int A = scanner.nextInt();
        System.out.print("Enter the value of B: ");
        int B = scanner.nextInt();

        int largestNumber;
        if (A > B) {
          largestNumber = A;
        }
        else {
          largestNumber = B;
        }

        System.out.println("The largest number is: " + largestNumber);

        scanner.close();
    }
}
```

# Checking Divisibility By 3

Checking if a given number N is divisible by 3.

## Understanding the Problem

The problem is to determine whether a given number N is divisible by 3. To solve this, we need to check if the remainder of dividing N by 3 is zero. If the remainder is zero, it means N is evenly divisible by 3. Otherwise, it is not divisible.

## Approach

To check if a number N is divisible by 3, we can follow a simple approach. We will use the modulo operator (%) in Java, which returns the remainder of dividing two numbers. By dividing N by 3 and checking if the remainder is zero, we can determine whether N is divisible by 3 or not.

**Step-by-Step Solution**

Let's break down the problem into steps:

Step 1: Accept the input value for N.

Step 2: Calculate the remainder by dividing N by 3 using the modulo operator (%).

Step 3: Check if the remainder is zero.

Step 4: If the remainder is zero, print that N is divisible by 3. Otherwise, print that N is not divisible by 3.

Now, let's translate our solution into code:

```
import java.util.Scanner;
public class DivisibleByThree {
    public static void main(String[] args) {
        Scanner scanner = new Scanner(System.in);

        // Step 1: Accept the input value for N
        System.out.print("Enter a number: ");
        int N = scanner.nextInt();

        // Step 2: Calculate the remainder
        int remainder = N % 3;

        // Step 3: Check if the remainder is zero
        if (remainder == 0) {
            // Step 4: Print that N is divisible by 3
            System.out.println(N + " is divisible by 3.");
        } else {
            // Step 4: Print that N is not divisible by 3
            System.out.println(N + " is not divisible by 3.");
        }

        // Step 5: End the program
        scanner.close();
    }
}
```

# Ternary Operator

The ternary operator, also known as the conditional operator, is a shorthand alternative to the traditional if-else statement. It allows us to evaluate a condition and choose between two expressions based on the result of that condition.

## Syntax

The syntax of the ternary operator is as follows:

```
condition ? expression1 : expression2
```

If the condition evaluates to true, expression1 is executed; otherwise, expression2 is executed. The result of the ternary operation is the value of the executed expression.

## Example Usage

Let's look at a simple example to illustrate the usage of the ternary operator. Consider a scenario where we want to determine whether a given number is positive or negative.

```
int number = -5;
String result = (number > 0) ? "Positive" : "Negative";
System.out.println("The number is " + result);
```

In this example, the condition (number > 0) is evaluated. If it is true, the expression "Positive" is assigned to the result variable;

otherwise, the expression “Negative” is assigned. Finally, the value of result is printed.

## Benefits of the Ternary Operator

1. Concise code: The ternary operator allows you to express conditional statements in a more compact and concise manner, reducing the number of lines of code.
2. Readability: With its intuitive syntax, the ternary operator improves code readability, making it easier for others to understand your logic.

While the ternary operator offers benefits, it is important to use it judiciously. Its simplicity can sometimes lead to overly complex expressions, reducing code readability. It is best suited for simple conditional statements and should not be used excessively or nested excessively to maintain code clarity.

Ch 18

# Determining Odd or Even

In this article, we will explore a simple and efficient approach to determine whether a number N is odd or even. By following the steps outlined below, you'll gain a clear understanding of how to tackle this problem effectively.

## Understanding the Problem

Before diving into the solution, let's quickly recap what it means for a number to be odd or even. An even number is divisible by 2, meaning it leaves no remainder when divided by 2. On the other hand, an odd number does leave a remainder of 1 when divided by 2.

## Approach

To check if a number N is odd or even, we can use the remainder of N divided by 2. If the remainder is 0, the number is even. If the remainder is 1, the number is odd.

## Steps

1. Accept the input number N.
2. Calculate the remainder by performing the operation N % 2. If the remainder is 0, the number is even. Otherwise, it is odd.
3. Print the result.

## Step-by-Step Solution

### Step 1: Accepting User Input

Let's start by writing a simple program to accept the input value for N:

```
import java.util.Scanner;

public class ParityChecker {
    public static void main(String[] args) {
        Scanner scanner = new Scanner(System.in);

        System.out.print("Enter a number: ");
        int N = scanner.nextInt();

        // More code to come!
    }
}
```

### Step 2: Calculating Remainder

To calculate the remainder, we'll use the modulo operator (%) in Java. Here's the code snippet to accomplish this:

```
int remainder = N % 2;
```

## Step 3: Printing the Result

Finally, let's check if the remainder is 0 or 1 and print the result. Here's the complete program:

```
import java.util.Scanner;

public class ParityChecker {
    public static void main(String[] args) {
        Scanner scanner = new Scanner(System.in);

        System.out.print("Enter a number: ");
        int N = scanner.nextInt();

        int remainder = N % 2;
        String parity = (remainder == 0) ? "even" : "odd";

        System.out.println("The number " + N + " is " + parity + ".");

        scanner.close();
    }
}
```

## Revision

**Given two numbers A and B, print the largest.**

1. Step 1: Accept the input values for A and B.
2. Step 2: Compare the values of A and B using an "if" statement.
3. Step 3: If A is greater than B, print A as the largest number. Otherwise, print B as the largest number.
4. Step 4: End the program.

**Given a number N, check if it is divisible by 3.**

1. Step 1: Accept the input value for N.
2. Step 2: Calculate the remainder by dividing N by 3 using the modulo operator (%).
3. Step 3: Check if the remainder is zero.
4. Step 4: If the remainder is zero, print that N is divisible by 3. Otherwise, print that N is not divisible by 3.
5. Step 5: End the program.

**What is the Ternary Operator**

The ternary operator, also known as the conditional operator, is a shorthand alternative to the traditional if-else statement in Java. It allows us to evaluate a condition and choose between two expressions based on the result of that condition.

Syntax: condition? expression1: expression2

Example: string result = (number >0)? "Positive": "Negative"

**<u>Given a number N, check if it is odd or even.</u>**

1. Step 1: Accept the input number N.
2. Step 2: Calculate the remainder by performing the operation N % 2.
3. Step 3: If the remainder is 0, the number is even. Otherwise, it is odd.
4. Step 4: Print the result.

Section 5

# Problem Solving Using Multiple if Statements

# Largest Among Three Numbers

Find the largest number among three given numbers.

## Understanding the Problem

The problem involves accepting three numbers as input and finding the largest among them. We need to compare the values of the three numbers and determine which one is the greatest.

## Approach

To solve this problem, we will use conditional statements to compare the three numbers and identify the largest one. We will utilize the if-else construct to handle the comparison and determine the maximum value.

**Step-by-Step Solution**

Step 1: Accepting User Input Start by accepting the three numbers as input from the user. You can use the Scanner class in Java to achieve this.

Step 2: Comparing the Numbers Using conditional statements, compare the three numbers to find the largest one. We will use the if-else construct to handle the comparison.

Step 3: Determining the Largest Number Within the if-else construct, compare the numbers using logical operators (>, <, >=, <=) to identify the largest value.

Step 4: Displaying the Result Finally, print the largest number to the user.

```
import java.util.Scanner;

public class LargestNumberFinder {
    public static void main(String[] args) {
        Scanner scanner = new Scanner(System.in);

        System.out.print("Enter the first number: ");
        int number1 = scanner.nextInt();

        System.out.print("Enter the second number: ");
        int number2 = scanner.nextInt();

        System.out.print("Enter the third number: ");
        int number3 = scanner.nextInt();

        int largestNumber;

        if (number1 >= number2 && number1 >= number3) {
            largestNumber = number1;
        } else if (number2 >= number1 && number2 >= number3) {
            largestNumber = number2;
        } else {
            largestNumber = number3;
        }

        System.out.println("The largest number is: " + largestNumber);

        scanner.close();
    }
}
```

# Finding Percentage and Grade

## Understanding the Problem

Calculating the percentage and assigning a grade based on the obtained marks is a common task in educational assessments. The problem involves accepting the obtained marks and total marks as input, calculating the percentage, and determining the grade based on the percentage. The grading scale may vary, but for this example, we will use a simple one with predefined ranges.

## Approach

To find the percentage, we divide the obtained marks by the total marks and multiply the result by 100: (Obtained Marks / Total Marks) * 100.

Based on the calculated percentage, we can assign a corresponding grade using conditional statements. For simplicity, let's assume a grading scale with the following ranges:

- 90% and above: A
- 80% - 89%: B
- 70% - 79%: C
- 60% - 69%: D
- Below 60%: F

## Step-by-Step Solution

### Step1: Accepting User Input

To gather the input from the user, we will use the Scanner class in Java. This class allows us to read input from various sources, such as the console.

### Step 2: Calculating the Percentage

Using the obtained marks and total marks, we can calculate the percentage by dividing the obtained marks by the total marks and multiplying the result by 100.

### Step 3: Determining the Grade

Based on the calculated percentage, we will assign a grade using conditional statements. The grading scale can vary, but for this example, we will assume the following ranges:

- 90% and above: A
- 80% - 89%: B
- 70% - 79%: C
- 60% - 69%: D
- Below 60%: F

### Step 4: Printing the Result

Finally, we will display the calculated percentage and assigned grade to the user.

## ➢ Finding Percentage and Grade ➣

```
import java.util.Scanner;

public class PercentageAndGradeCalculator {
    public static void main(String[] args) {
        Scanner scanner = new Scanner(System.in);

        System.out.print("Enter the obtained marks: ");
        double obtainedMarks = scanner.nextDouble();

        System.out.print("Enter the total marks: ");
        double totalMarks = scanner.nextDouble();

        double percentage = (obtainedMarks / totalMarks) * 100;

        String grade;

        if (percentage >= 90) {
            grade = "A";
        } else if (percentage >= 80) {
            grade = "B";
        } else if (percentage >= 70) {
            grade = "C";
        } else if (percentage >= 60) {
            grade = "D";
        } else {
            grade = "F";
        }

        System.out.println("Percentage: " + percentage + "%");
        System.out.println("Grade: " + grade);

        scanner.close();
    }
}
```

# Calculating Water Bill

## Introduction

In this article, we will explore how to calculate a water bill with an increasing rate per unit based on consumption. Many utility companies charge higher rates as the water consumption increases, which requires a dynamic calculation. By following the step-by-step solution provided in this article, you will be able to calculate the water bill, taking into account the varying rates per unit.

## Understanding the Problem

The problem involves calculating the water bill based on the water consumption and the increasing rate per unit. We need to consider the consumption levels and apply the appropriate rate to calculate the total bill.

## Approach

To solve this problem, we will use conditional statements to determine the applicable rate per unit based on the consumption level. We will then multiply the consumption by the corresponding rate and calculate the total bill.

**Step-by-Step Solution:**

### Step 1: Accepting User Input

Start by accepting the water consumption from the user. You can use the Scanner class in Java to achieve this.

## Step 2: Determining the Applicable Rate per Unit

Using conditional statements, determine the rate per unit based on the consumption level. You will need to define the rate brackets and their corresponding rates.

## Step 3: Calculating the Water Bill

Multiply the consumption by the applicable rate per unit to calculate the cost for each bracket. Sum up the costs for all the brackets to obtain the total bill.

## Step 4: Displaying the Result

Finally, print the total bill to the user.

Now, let's put the steps into code and solve the problem:

```java
import java.util.Scanner;

public class WaterBillCalculator {
    public static void main(String[] args) {
        Scanner scanner = new Scanner(System.in);

        System.out.print("Enter the water consumption in cubic meters: ");
        double consumption = scanner.nextDouble();

        double ratePerUnit;

        if (consumption <= 10) {
            ratePerUnit = 5.0;
        } else if (consumption <= 20) {
            ratePerUnit = 7.5;
        } else if (consumption <= 30) {
            ratePerUnit = 10.0;
        } else {
            ratePerUnit = 12.5;
        }

        double totalBill = consumption * ratePerUnit;

        System.out.println("Water Bill: $" + totalBill);

        scanner.close();
    }
}
```

# Calculate Days in a Given Month

## Introduction

In this article, we will explore how to solve the problem of calculating the number of days in a given month.

## Understanding the Problem

The problem involves accepting a month as input and calculating the number of days in that month. We need to account for leap years, as the number of days in February varies based on whether it is a leap year or not.

## Approach

To solve this problem, we will use an if-else conditional statement to determine the number of days based on the input month. We will consider the specific cases of February in leap years and non-leap years. For the other months, we will use predefined values to determine the number of days.

**Step-by-Step Solution**

## Step 1: Accepting User Input

We will start by accepting the month as input from the user. You can use the Scanner class in Java to achieve this.

## Step 2: Determining the Number of Days

Next, we will determine the number of days based on the input month. We will use an if-else conditional statement to handle the different cases.

## Step 3: Handling February in Leap Years

For February, we need to check if the year is a leap year. If it is, the number of days will be 29; otherwise, it will be 28. We will discuss how to find leap year in next chapter.

## Step 4: Handling the Remaining Months

For the other months, we can use predefined values to determine the number of days. For example, January, March, May, July, August, October, and December have 31 days, while April, June, September, and November have 30 days.

## Code Implementation

Now, let's put the steps into code and solve the problem:

## ➢ Calculate Days in a Given Month ➣

```
import java.util.Scanner;

public class DaysInMonthCalculator {
    public static void main(String[] args) {
        Scanner scanner = new Scanner(System.in);

        System.out.print("Enter the month (1-12): ");
        int month = scanner.nextInt();

        int days;

        if (month == 2) {
            System.out.print("Enter the year: ");
            int year = scanner.nextInt();

            if ((year % 4 == 0 && year % 100 != 0) || year % 400 == 0) {
                days = 29; // Leap year
            } else {
                days = 28; // Non-leap year
            }
        } else if (month == 4 || month == 6 || month == 9 || month == 11) {
            days = 30; // April, June, September, November
        } else {
            days = 31; // January, March, May, July, August, October, December
        }

        System.out.println("Number of days in the given month: " + days);

        scanner.close();
    }
}
```

We can also use switch statements to solve these types of problems as they provide an alternative to long chains of if-else statements.

```
import java.util.Scanner;
public class DaysInMonthCalculator {
    public static void main(String[] args) {
        Scanner scanner = new Scanner(System.in);
        System.out.print("Enter the month (1-12): ");
        int month = scanner.nextInt();
        System.out.print("Enter the year: ");
        int year = scanner.nextInt();
        int daysInMonth = 0;
        switch (month) {
            case 1: // January
            case 3: // March
            case 5: // May
            case 7: // July
            case 8: // August
            case 10: // October
            case 12: // December
                daysInMonth = 31;
                break;
            case 4: // April
            case 6: // June
            case 9: // September
            case 11: // November
                daysInMonth = 30;
                break;
            case 2: // February
                if ((year % 4 == 0 && year % 100 != 0) || (year % 400 == 0)) {
                    daysInMonth = 29; // Leap year
                } else {
                    daysInMonth = 28; // Non-leap year
                }
                break;
            default:
                System.out.println("Invalid month!");
        }
        if (daysInMonth != 0) {
            System.out.println("Number of days in the given month: " + daysInMonth);
        }
        scanner.close();
    }
}
```

Ch 23

# Solving the Leap Year Problem

The leap year problem is a common programming task that involves determining whether a given year is a leap year or not. In this chapter, we will explore the understanding, approach, step-by-step solution, and code to solve the leap year problem.

## Understanding the Problem

A leap year is a year that is divisible by 4, except for end-of-century years (years ending in '00'), which are leap years only if they are also divisible by 400. For example, 2000 was a leap year because it is divisible by 400, whereas 1900 was not a leap year because although it is divisible by 4, it is also a century year not divisible by 400.

## Approach

To solve the leap year problem, we can

- Take the year as input.
- Check if the year is divisible by 4.
- If it is divisible by 4, check if it is a century year (ends with '00').
- If it is a century year, check if it is divisible by 400.

If it is divisible by 4, it is a leap year. But if it is divisible by 100 and not by 400, then it is not a leap year

## Step-by-Step Solution

### Step 1: Accepting User Input

The code begins by importing the Scanner class from java.util package, which is used for taking input from the user.

The LeapYear class contains a main method, which is the entry point of the program. Inside the main method:

- It creates a new Scanner object named scanner to read input from the console.
- Asks the user to enter a year by displaying the message "Enter a year: ".
- Reads the integer input provided by the user and stores it in the variable year.

### Step 2: Determine if the input year is a leap year or not

main method calls the isLeapYear method with the input year as an argument to check if it's a leap year or not.

The isLeapYear method takes an integer year as input and returns a Boolean value (true if the year is a leap year, false otherwise).

- It checks if the input year is divisible by 4 using the condition year % 4 == 0. If true, it proceeds to the next step.
    - If the year is divisible by 4, it checks if it's also divisible by 100 using the condition year % 100 == 0.
        - If true, it further checks if the year is divisible by 400 using the condition year % 400 == 0.
            - If all conditions (year % 4 == 0, year % 100 == 0, year % 400 == 0) are true, it returns true, indicating that the year is a leap year.

    - If the year is not divisible by 400, it returns false, indicating that the year is not a leap year.
- If the year is not divisible by 4, the method directly returns false, indicating that the year is not a leap year.

## Step 3: Print the result

print the result based on the return value of isLeapYear.

Let's implement this approach:

```java
import java.util.Scanner;
public class LeapYear {
    public static void main(String[] args) {
        Scanner scanner = new Scanner(System.in);
        System.out.print("Enter a year: ");
        int year = scanner.nextInt();

        if (isLeapYear(year)) {
            System.out.println(year + " is a leap year.");
        } else {
            System.out.println(year + " is not a leap year.");
        }
        scanner.close();
    }
    public static boolean isLeapYear(int year) {
        if (year % 4 == 0) {
            if (year % 100 == 0) {
                if(year % 400 == 0){
                   return true;
                }
                else {
                   return false;
                }
            }
            else {
                return true;
            }
        }
        else {
            return false;
        }
    }
}
```

## Revision

### Largest among Three Numbers

1. Accepting User Input Start by accepting the three numbers as input from the user. You can use the Scanner class in Java to achieve this.
2. Comparing the Numbers Using conditional statements, compare the three numbers to find the largest one. We will use the if-else construct to handle the comparison.
3. Determining the Largest Number Within the if-else construct, compare the numbers using logical operators (>, <, >=, <=) to identify the largest value.
4. Displaying the Result Finally, print the largest number to the user.

### Find Percentage and Grade

1. Accept the obtained marks and total marks as input from the user.
2. Calculate the percentage using the formula: (obtainedMarks / totalMarks) * 100.
3. Determine the grade based on the percentage using conditional statements.
4. Print the calculated percentage and assigned grade to the user.

### Calculating Water Bill

1. Start by accepting the water consumption from the user. You can use the Scanner class in Java to achieve this.

2. Using conditional statements, determine the rate per unit based on the consumption level. You will need to define the rate brackets and their corresponding rates.
3. Multiply the consumption by the applicable rate per unit to calculate the cost for each bracket. Sum up the costs for all the brackets to obtain the total bill.
4. Finally, print the total bill to the user.

## Calculating Days in a Given Month

1. We will start by accepting the month as input from the user. You can use the Scanner class in Java to achieve this.
2. Next, we will determine the number of days based on the input month. We will use an if-else conditional statement to handle the different cases.
3. For February, we need to check if the year is a leap year. If it is, the number of days will be 29; otherwise, it will be 28.
4. For the other months, we can use predefined values to determine the number of days. For example, January, March, May, July, August, October, and December have 31 days, while April, June, September, and November have 30 days.

Section 6

# Iterations

# Increment and Decrement Operators

Before we begin with iterations let's strengthen our understanding of Increment and decrement operators. Although they are not directly linked with iterations but are widely used in loops. Increment and decrement operators are fundamental tools in programming languages that allow you to modify the value of a variable by incrementing or decrementing it by a specific amount. These operators are commonly used in loops, arithmetic calculations, and other scenarios where you need to update a variable's value. In this article, we will explore the increment and decrement operators in detail, understand their behaviour, and provide examples to demonstrate their usage.

## Increment Operator (++)

The increment operator (++) is used to increase the value of a variable by 1. It can be applied to both numeric and character variables. The operator can be placed before the variable (pre-increment) or after the variable (post-increment). The behaviour of the operator differs depending on its placement.

**Pre-increment (++variable):** In pre-increment, the variable is incremented first, and then its updated value is used in the expression where it appears.

**Post-increment (variable++):** In post-increment, the variable is used in the expression where it appears, and then its value is incremented.

```
int x = 5;
int y = ++x; // pre-increment: x is incremented to 6, and y is assigned the value 6
System.out.println("x: " + x); // Output: 6
System.out.println("y: " + y); // Output: 6

int a = 10;
int b = a++; // post-increment: b is assigned the initial value of a (10), and then a is
incremented to 11
System.out.println("a: " + a); // Output: 11
System.out.println("b: " + b); // Output: 10
```

## Decrement Operator (--)

The decrement operator (--) is similar to the increment operator but decreases the value of a variable by 1. It follows the same pre-decrement (--) and post-decrement (--) syntax as the increment operator.

```
int p = 8;
int q = --p; // pre-decrement: p is decremented to 7, and q is assigned the value 7
System.out.println("p: " + p); // Output: 7
System.out.println("q: " + q); // Output: 7

int m = 15;
int n = m--; // post-decrement: n is assigned the initial value of m (15), and then m is
decremented to 14
System.out.println("m: " + m); // Output: 14
System.out.println("n: " + n); // Output: 15
```

# Ch 25

## While Loop

In programming, the while loop is a control flow statement that allows a block of code to be repeatedly executed as long as a specified condition remains true. It provides an effective way to create loops that continue until a particular condition is no longer met. In this chapter, we will explore the while loop, discussing its syntax, functionality, and practical examples to help you grasp its concept and unleash its potential in your programs.

### Understanding the While Loop

The while loop is a pre-test loop, meaning that it evaluates the condition before executing the code block. If the condition is true, the code block is executed, and the loop continues until the condition becomes false. The general structure of a while loop is as follows:

```
while (condition) {
    // Code to be executed
}
```

### Approach

To effectively use the while loop, follow these steps:

1. Initialize variables and define the initial conditions.
2. Write the while loop with the condition that needs to be evaluated.

3. Within the loop, include the code block that you want to repeat.
4. Update variables within the loop to avoid infinite looping.
5. Ensure the loop condition will eventually become false to exit the loop.

**Step-by-Step Solution**

**Step 1: Initialization**

Start by initializing a variable that will serve as the loop counter and any other relevant variables needed in your code.

**Step 2: While Loop Structure**

Write the while loop, specifying the condition that needs to be evaluated. This condition should be based on the task or requirement you want to accomplish.

**Step 3: Code Execution**

Within the while loop, write the code block that you want to repeat until the condition becomes false. This code block can include any valid Java statements, such as calculations, input/output operations, or conditional logic.

**Step 4: Variable Update**

To prevent an infinite loop, ensure that the variables within the loop are updated with each iteration. This update can involve incrementing or decrementing the loop counter, modifying other variables, or utilizing conditional statements to control the loop flow.

## Step 5: Exit Condition

Ensure that the loop condition will eventually become false, allowing the program to exit the loop and continue with the rest of the code.

```
public class Countdown {
    public static void main(String[] args) {
        int count = 10; // Starting count

        while (count >= 1) {
            System.out.println(count);
            count--;
        }
    }
}
```

Ch 26

# DO-While Loop

The do-while loop is a control flow statement that allows a block of code to be repeatedly executed until a specified condition is no longer true. It differs from the while loop in that it guarantees at least one execution of the code block, as the condition is checked at the end of each iteration. In this chapter, we will explore the do-while loop, discussing its syntax, functionality, and practical examples to help you grasp its concept and leverage its power in your programs.

## Understanding the Do-While Loop

The do-while loop is a post-test loop, meaning that it executes the code block first and then checks the condition. If the condition evaluates to true, the loop continues execution, and the code block is repeated. The general structure of a do-while loop is as follows:

```
do {
    // Code to be executed
} while (condition);
```

## Approach

To effectively use the do-while loop, follow these steps:

1. Initialize variables and define the initial conditions.
2. Write the do-while loop with the code block you want to execute.
3. Ensure the loop block will modify the variables involved in the loop condition.

4. Specify the condition to be evaluated at the end of each iteration.
5. Continue loop execution as long as the condition remains true.

**Step-by-Step Solution**

**Step 1: Initialization**

Start by initializing any required variables and defining the initial conditions for your program.

**Step 2: Do-While Loop Structure**

Write the do-while loop, enclosing the code block you want to execute within the loop. Ensure the code block modifies the variables involved in the loop condition.

**Step 3: Code Execution**

Within the do-while loop, include the code block you want to repeat until the condition becomes false. This block can contain any valid Java statements, such as calculations, input/output operations, or conditional logic.

**Step 4: Condition Evaluation**

Specify the condition to be evaluated at the end of each iteration. This condition determines whether the loop will continue executing or terminate.

## Step 5: Loop Execution

Continue loop execution as long as the condition remains true. If the condition evaluates to false, the loop terminates, and program execution continues with the next statement outside the loop.

## Example: Counting Up with a Do-While Loop

Let's consider an example where we use a do-while loop to count up from 1 to a given number.

```
public class CountingUp {
    public static void main(String[] args) {
        int count = 1; // Starting count

        do {
            System.out.println(count);
            count++;
        } while (count <= 10);
    }
}
```

# For Loop

The **for loop** is a powerful control flow statement that allows repetitive execution of a block of code based on a defined set of conditions. It provides a concise and efficient way to iterate over a range of values or perform a task a specific number of times. In this chapter, we will delve into the for loop, exploring its syntax, functionality, and practical examples to help you understand and harness its capabilities in your programs.

## Understanding the for Loop

The for loop is a versatile construct that combines the initialization, condition, and update of loop variables within a single line. It iterates over a specified range or collection of values, executing the code block until the condition becomes false. The general structure of a for loop is as follows:

```
for (initialization; condition; update) {
    // Code to be executed
}
```

## Approach

To effectively use the for loop, follow these steps:

1. Initialize variables and define the initial conditions.
2. Specify the loop condition that determines when the loop will continue executing.
3. Include the code block you want to repeat within the loop.

4. Define the update statement that modifies the loop variables in each iteration.
5. Continue loop execution until the condition becomes false.

**Step-by-Step Solution**

**Step 1: Initialization**

Start by initializing any required variables and defining the initial conditions for your loop.

**Step 2: For Loop Structure**

Write the for loop, including the initialization, condition, and update statements within the parentheses. Ensure that the loop variables are set up correctly.

**Step 3: Code Execution**

Within the for loop, include the code block that you want to repeat until the condition becomes false. This block can contain any valid Java statements, such as calculations, input/output operations, or conditional logic.

**Step 4: Variable Update**

Define the update statement that modifies the loop variables in each iteration. This statement can involve incrementing or decrementing loop counters, modifying other variables, or utilizing conditional statements to control the loop flow.

**Step 5: Condition Evaluation**

Continue loop execution until the condition specified in the for loop becomes false. If the condition evaluates to false, the loop terminates, and program execution continues with the next statement outside the loop.

## Example: Printing Numbers with a For Loop

Let's consider an example where we use a for loop to print the numbers from 1 to 10.

```
public class NumberPrinter {
    public static void main(String[] args) {
        for (int i = 1; i <= 10; i++) {
            System.out.println(i);
        }
    }
}
```

# Break and Continue Statements

The **break** and **continue** statements are essential tools for controlling the flow of execution within loops. These statements provide flexibility and control by allowing you to alter the normal behaviour of loops based on specific conditions. In this chapter, we will delve into the break and continue statements, explaining their purpose, illustrating their usage with examples, and discussing their impact on loop execution.

**break**

The break statement is used to immediately exit a loop, regardless of whether the loop condition is still true. It is commonly used to terminate a loop prematurely when a certain condition is met. When encountered, the break statement causes the program to exit the loop entirely and continue with the next statement after the loop.

**Example 1: Using break in a for loop**

```
for (int i = 1; i <= 10; i++) {
    if (i == 5) {
        break; // Terminate the loop when i equals 5
    }
    System.out.println(i);
}
```

**Output**

1

2

3

4

In this example, the loop starts from 1 and increments by 1. When i becomes 5, the break statement is encountered, causing the loop to terminate immediately. The program then proceeds to the next statement after the loop.

**continue**

The continue statement is used to skip the current iteration of a loop and move on to the next iteration. It allows you to bypass the remaining code within the loop for a particular iteration, but the loop continues executing with the next iteration. The continue statement is typically used when you want to skip certain iterations based on specific conditions.

**Example 2: Using continue in a while loop**

```
int i = 0;
while (i < 10) {
    i++;
    if (i % 2 == 0) {
        continue; // Skip even numbers
    }
    System.out.println(i);
}
```

**Output**

1

3

5

7

9

In this example, the while loop is set to iterate as long as i is less than 10. Inside the loop, the continue statement is encountered when i is even. This causes the program to skip the remaining code within the loop and move on to the next iteration.

## Revision

### Increment and Decrement Operators

- The increment operator (++) is used to increase the value of a variable by 1. It can be applied to both numeric and character variables.

  1. **Pre-increment (++variable):** In pre-increment, the variable is incremented first, and then its updated value is used in the expression where it appears.
  2. **Post-increment (variable++):** In post-increment, the variable is used in the expression where it appears, and then its value is incremented.

- The decrement operator (--) is similar to the increment operator but decreases the value of a variable by 1. It follows the same pre-decrement (--) and post-decrement (--) syntax as the increment operator.

### While Loop

```
public class Countdown {
    public static void main(String[] args) {
        int count = 10; // Starting count

        while (count >= 1) {
            System.out.println(count);
            count--;
        }
    }
}
```

## Do-While Loop

```
public class CountingUp {
    public static void main(String[] args) {
        int count = 1; // Starting count

        do {
            System.out.println(count);
            count++;
        } while (count <= 10);
    }
}
```

## For Loop

```
public class NumberPrinter {
    public static void main(String[] args) {
        for (int i = 1; i <= 10; i++) {
            System.out.println(i);
        }
    }
}
```

## Break and Continue

The break statement is used to immediately exit a loop, regardless of whether the loop condition is still true.

```
for (int i = 1; i <= 10; i++) {
    if (i == 5) {
        break; // Terminate the loop when i equals 5
    }
    System.out.println(i);
}
```

The continue statement is used to skip the current iteration of a loop and move on to the next iteration.

```
int i = 0;
while (i < 10) {
    i++;
    if (i % 2 == 0) {
        continue; // Skip even numbers
    }
    System.out.println(i);
}
```

Section 7

# Problem Solving Using Loops

Ch 29

# Find the Nth Power of 2

## Introduction

In the realm of mathematics and computer programming, exponentiation plays a crucial role in various calculations and algorithms. In this chapter, we will explore the concept of finding the Nth power of 2, providing a comprehensive understanding of the process, the approach to tackle it, and step-by-step solutions with code examples.

## Understanding the Nth Power of 2

The Nth power of 2 is obtained by multiplying 2 by itself N times. For example, $2^3$ represents the $3^{rd}$ power of 2, which equals $2 \times 2 \times 2 = 8$. The power of 2 grows exponentially as N increases, showcasing the remarkable growth of powers of 2 in binary representations and other mathematical operations.

## Approach

To find the Nth power of 2, we can adopt a simple and efficient approach:

1. Initialize a variable, say result, with the value 1, representing the base case where $2^0$ equals 1.
2. Use a loop structure, such as a for loop, to iterate N times.
3. Multiply the current value of result by 2 in each iteration.

4. After completing the loop, the value of result will hold the Nth power of 2.

**Step-by-Step Solution**

**Step 1: Initialization**

Start by initializing the result variable with the value 1, representing the base case.

**Step 2: Loop Structure**

Use a loop structure, such as a for loop, to iterate N times. Set up the loop to run from 1 to N inclusive.

**Step 3: Multiplication**

Within each iteration, multiply the current value of result by 2, updating the result variable.

**Step 4: Loop Execution**

Continue loop execution until the loop reaches the Nth iteration.

**Step 5: Final Result**

After completing the loop, the value of result will hold the Nth power of 2.

**Example: Finding the 6th Power of 2**

Let's consider an example where we find the 6th power of 2 using the approach described above.

## ➢ Find the Nth Power of 2 ➣

```
public class PowerOfTwo {
    public static void main(String[] args) {
        int N = 6;
        int result = 1;

        for (int i = 1; i <= N; i++) {
            result *= 2;
        }

        System.out.println("The 6th power of 2 is: " + result);
    }
}
```

**Output**

The 6th power of 2 is: 64

# Find GCD By Iteration

## Introduction

In the realm of number theory and algorithmic problem-solving, finding the Greatest Common Divisor (GCD) holds paramount importance. The GCD also known as HCF (Highest common factor) represents the largest positive integer that divides two or more numbers without leaving a remainder. In this chapter, we will delve into the concept of finding the GCD by iteration, providing a comprehensive understanding, an effective approach, and a step-by-step solution with code examples.

## Understanding the GCD

The Greatest Common Divisor (GCD) of two numbers is the largest positive integer that divides both numbers evenly. It represents a fundamental concept in number theory and is widely used in various mathematical calculations, including simplifying fractions, prime factorization, and solving modular equations.

## Approach

To find the GCD of two numbers by iteration, we can adopt a simple and intuitive approach. The steps involved are as follows:

1. Start with two given numbers, let's say A and B.
2. Iterate from 1 to the smaller of the two numbers.
3. Check if the current number divides both A and B without leaving a remainder.

4. Keep track of the largest number that satisfies the above condition.
5. The largest number found in the iteration represents the GCD of the original two numbers.

**Step-by-Step Solution**

**Step 1: Input Numbers**

Start by obtaining the two numbers, A and B, for which you want to find the GCD.

**Step 2: Determine the Smaller Number**

Compare the values of A and B to identify the smaller number.

**Step 3: Iterate from 1 to the Smaller Number**

Use a loop structure, such as a for loop, to iterate from 1 to the smaller number inclusive.

**Step 4: Check for Divisibility**

Within each iteration, check if the current number divides both A and B without leaving a remainder. Use the modulus operator (%) to perform this check.

**Step 5: Track the Largest Divisor**

If the current number divides both A and B without leaving a remainder, update a variable, let's call it gcd, to store the largest divisor found so far.

**Step 6: Loop Execution**

Continue the loop until it reaches the end of the iteration range.

## Step 7: Final Result

After completing the loop, the value of gcd will hold the GCD of the original two numbers.

## Example: Finding the GCD of 36 and 48

Let's consider an example where we find the GCD of 36 and 48 using the iteration approach.

```
public class GCD {
    public static int findGCD(int A, int B) {
        int smaller = Math.min(A, B);
        int gcd = 1;

        for (int i = 1; i <= smaller; i++) {
            if (A % i == 0 && B % i == 0) {
                gcd = i;
            }
        }

        return gcd;
    }

    public static void main(String[] args) {
        int number1 = 36;
        int number2 = 48;
        int gcd = findGCD(number1, number2);
        System.out.println("The GCD of " + number1 + " and " + number2 + " is: " + gcd);
    }
}
```

## Output

The GCD of 36 and 48 is: 12

By employing iteration and checking for divisibility, we can efficiently compute the GCD of two numbers, providing a crucial tool for various mathematical calculations and problem-solving scenarios.

The GCD algorithm by iteration is straightforward and can be extended to larger numbers as well. Experiment with different inputs, explore further applications of the GCD, and leverage this knowledge to solve more complex mathematical problems.

# Ch 31

# Prime Number Checker

## Introduction

Prime numbers are those that have exactly two distinct positive divisors: 1 and the number itself. In this article, we will explore the concept of prime numbers, provide a comprehensive understanding, an effective approach, and a step-by-step solution with code examples to solve the problem of determining if a number is prime.

## Understanding Prime Numbers

Prime numbers are fundamental elements in number theory and have intrigued mathematicians for centuries. They are defined as positive integers greater than 1 that have no divisors other than 1 and the number itself. Prime numbers possess unique properties and play a significant role in various mathematical computations, cryptography, and algorithmic problem-solving.

## Approach

To determine if a given number N is prime, we can adopt a straightforward and efficient approach. The steps involved are as follows:

1. Start with the given number N.
2. Iterate from 2 to N - 1.
3. Check if any number within the iteration range divides N without leaving a remainder.

4. If a divisor is found, the number is not prime.
5. If no divisor is found, the number is prime.

**Step-by-Step Solution**

**Step 1: Input Number**

Start by obtaining the number N for which you want to determine if it is prime.

**Step 2: Iteration Range**

Set up a loop structure, such as a for loop, to iterate from 2 to N - 1.

**Step 3: Check for Divisibility**

Within each iteration, check if the current number divides N without leaving a remainder. Use the modulus operator (%) to perform this check.

**Step 4: Prime or Not Prime**

If a divisor is found, the number is not prime. Exit the loop and conclude that the number is not prime. If no divisor is found after the entire iteration, the number is prime.

**Step 5: Final Result**

Output the result indicating whether the number is prime or not.

**Example: Determining if a Number is Prime**

Let's consider an example where we determine if the number 17 is prime using the above approach.

```
public class PrimeNumberChecker {
    public static boolean isPrime(int N) {
        if (N <= 1) {
            return false;
        }

        for (int i = 2; i <= N-1; i++) {
            if (N % i == 0) {
                return false;
            }
        }

        return true;
    }

    public static void main(String[] args) {
        int number = 17;
        boolean isPrime = isPrime(number);
        if (isPrime) {
            System.out.println(number + " is a prime number.");
        } else {
            System.out.println(number + " is not a prime number.");
        }
    }
}
```

**Output**

17 is a prime number.

Ch 32

# Finding Prime Numbers From 1 to N Using Iterations

## Introduction

Prime numbers are an essential concept in number theory and have numerous applications in various fields, including computer science and cryptography. In this chapter, we will explore an iterative approach to solving this problem. We will discuss the understanding, approach, step-by-step solution, and provide sample code to illustrate the process.

Approach

The iterative approach to finding prime numbers from 1 to N involves checking each number in the range to determine if it is prime or not. To do this, we need to iterate through each number and verify if it is only divisible by 1 and itself. The approach is straightforward and can be optimized to some extent by reducing the number of iterations.

### Step-by-Step Solution

1. Input the value of N, which represents the upper limit of the range.
2. Iterate through each number from 2 to N
3. For each number, check if it is divisible by any number from 2 to the square root of the number (inclusive). If there is a divisor greater than square root of number then there will also be a divisor less than the square root of the number.

So, iterating till square root of number will be sufficient for validating if a number is prime or not

4. If it is divisible by any number other than 1 and itself, it is not a prime number. Move to the next number.
5. If it is not divisible by any number other than 1 and itself, it is a prime number. Output the number as one of the prime numbers in the range.

Here's an example implementation for finding prime numbers from 1 to N using iterations:

```
import java.util.*;

public class PrimeNumbers {
    public static void main(String[] args) {
        Scanner scanner = new Scanner(System.in);

        System.out.print("Enter the value of N: ");
        int N = scanner.nextInt();

        System.out.println("Prime numbers from 1 to " + N + ":");
        for (int i = 2; i <= N; i++) {
            boolean isPrime = true;
            for (int j = 2; j * j <= i; j++) {
                if (i % j == 0) {
                    isPrime = false;
                    break;
                }
            }
            if (isPrime) {
                System.out.print(i + " ");
            }
        }
    }
}
```

## Revision

### Nth Power of 2

1. Start by initializing the result variable with the value 1, representing the base case.
2. Use a loop structure, such as a for loop, to iterate N times. Set up the loop to run from 1 to N inclusive.
3. Within each iteration, multiply the current value of result by 2, updating the result variable.
4. Continue loop execution until the loop reaches the Nth iteration.
5. After completing the loop, the value of result will hold the Nth power of 2.

### GCD by iteration

1. Start by obtaining the two numbers, A and B, for which you want to find the GCD.
2. Compare the values of A and B to identify the smaller number. This will be crucial in determining the range of the iteration.
3. Use a loop structure, such as a for loop, to iterate from 1 to the smaller number inclusive.
4. Within each iteration, check if the current number divides both A and B without leaving a remainder. Use the modulus operator (%) to perform this check.
5. If the current number divides both A and B without leaving a remainder, update a variable, let's call it gcd, to store the largest divisor found so far.
6. Continue the loop until it reaches the end of the iteration range.

7. After completing the loop, the value of gcd will hold the GCD of the original two numbers.

**Prime Number Checker**

1. Start by obtaining the number N for which you want to determine if it is prime.
2. Set up a loop structure, such as a for loop, to iterate from 2 to N - 1.
3. Within each iteration, check if the current number divides N without leaving a remainder. Use the modulus operator (%) to perform this check.
4. If a divisor is found, the number is not prime. Exit the loop and conclude that the number is not prime. If no divisor is found after the entire iteration, the number is prime.
5. Output the result indicating whether the number is prime or not.

**Finding Prime Numbers from 1 to N Using Iterations**

1. Input the value of N, which represents the upper limit of the range.
2. Iterate through each number from 2 to N:
3. For each number, check if it is divisible by any number from 2 to the square root of the number (inclusive). If there is a divisor greater than square root of number then there will also be a divisor less than the square root of the number. So, iterating till square root of number will be sufficient for validating if a number is prime or not

4. If it is divisible by any number other than 1 and itself, it is not a prime number. Move to the next number.
5. If it is not divisible by any number other than 1 and itself, it is a prime number. Output the number as one of the prime numbers in the range.

Section 8

# Code Locally on Your Machine

Ch 33

# How to Compile and Run a Java Program Locally

## Introduction

Java is a widely used programming language known for its versatility and portability. To bring a Java program to life, you need to compile it into bytecode and then run it using the Java Virtual Machine (JVM). In this article, we will walk you through the process of compiling and running a Java program, providing a step-by-step guide to help you get started.

## Step 1: Install Java Development Kit (JDK)

Before you begin, ensure that you have the Java Development Kit (JDK) installed on your system. The JDK includes the Java compiler (javac) and other tools necessary for compiling and running Java programs. You can download the JDK from the official Oracle website: **https://www.oracle.com/java/technologies/javase-jdk11-downloads.html** and follow the installation instructions for your operating system.

## Step 2: Write Your Java Program

Using a text editor or an integrated development environment (IDE) like IntelliJ IDEA or Eclipse, write your Java program. Begin by creating a new Java source file with a.java extension. Make sure to define a class with a main() method, as it serves as the entry point for program execution. Add your desired code within the main() method to implement the functionality of your program.

### Step 3: Save Your Java Program

Save your Java program with a.java file extension. It is good practice to use a meaningful and descriptive filename that reflects the purpose of your program. For example, if you are creating a program to calculate the area of a circle, you could name your file CircleArea.java.

### Step 4: Open a Terminal or Command Prompt

To compile and run your Java program, you will need to use a terminal or command prompt. Open a terminal window on macOS or Linux, or a command prompt on Windows.

### Step 5: Navigate to the Program Directory

Using the terminal or command prompt, navigate to the directory where your Java program is saved. You can use the 'cd' command to change directories. For example, if your program is saved on the desktop, you can navigate to it by running:

```
cd Desktop
```

### Step 6: Compile Your Java Program

To compile your Java program, use the javac command followed by the name of your Java source file. For example, if your program is named CircleArea.java, run the following command:

```
javac CircleArea.java
```

If there are no syntax errors in your program, the Java compiler will generate a bytecode file named CircleArea.class.

## Step 7: Run Your Java Program

Once your Java program has been successfully compiled, you can run it using the java command followed by the name of the class containing the main() method. For example, if your main class is CircleArea, run the following command:

```
java CircleArea
```

The JVM will execute your Java program, and if all goes well, you will see the output in the terminal or command prompt.

Ch 34

# Essential Java Development Tools

Java is a versatile programming language used to develop a wide range of applications, from desktop software to web applications and mobile apps. To streamline the development process and enhance productivity, developers rely on various tools specifically designed for Java. In this chapter, we will explore some of the essential Java development tools, discussing their features, benefits, and use cases.

## Integrated Development Environments (IDEs)

IDEs are comprehensive software tools that provide an integrated environment for Java development. They offer features such as code editors, syntax highlighting, code completion, debugging tools, and project management capabilities. Some popular Java IDEs include:

- Eclipse: Eclipse is a widely used open-source IDE known for its extensibility and rich ecosystem of plugins. It offers advanced features for Java development, including refactoring tools, debugging support, and a powerful plugin architecture.
- IntelliJ IDEA: IntelliJ IDEA is a commercial IDE developed by JetBrains. It offers a user-friendly interface, intelligent code completion, advanced refactoring tools, built-in version control, and extensive support for various frameworks and technologies.

- NetBeans: NetBeans is an open-source IDE supported by the Apache Foundation. It provides a seamless development experience with features like smart code editing, easy project management, and support for multiple languages and frameworks.

## Build Tools

Build tools automate the process of compiling source code, managing dependencies, and creating executable files or deployable artifacts. They simplify project building, testing, and deployment. The most popular build tools for Java are:

- Apache Maven: Maven is a widely used build automation tool that focuses on project structure and dependency management. It uses XML-based configuration files (POM) to define project settings and dependencies, making it easy to manage complex projects.
- Gradle: Gradle is a flexible build automation tool that combines the features of Apache Ant and Maven. It uses a Groovy-based DSL (Domain-Specific Language) for build script configuration, allowing developers to write concise and expressive build scripts.

## Version Control Systems (VCS)

VCS tools enable developers to track changes to their codebase, collaborate with team members, and revert to previous versions if needed. The most popular VCS tools for Java development are:

- Git: Git is a distributed version control system known for its speed and flexibility. It allows developers to track changes, create branches for parallel development, merge code, and collaborate with other developers using platforms like GitHub or GitLab.

- Subversion (SVN): Subversion is a centralized version control system that offers features such as branching, merging, and tagging. It provides a centralized repository for code storage and collaboration.

## Testing Frameworks

Testing is an integral part of software development, and Java offers several powerful testing frameworks. Some widely used testing frameworks include:

Junit: JUnit is a popular unit testing framework for Java. It provides a simple and easy-to-use API for writing and executing tests. JUnit facilitates test-driven development (TDD) and supports features like test suites, annotations, and assertions.

TestNG: TestNG is an advanced testing framework that offers additional features beyond what JUnit provides. It supports parallel test execution, data-driven testing, test configuration through XML files, and flexible test grouping.

## Profiling and Debugging Tools

Profiling and debugging tools help developers identify and resolve performance issues, memory leaks, and other bugs in their Java applications. Some commonly used tools include:

Java VisualVM: Java VisualVM is a powerful profiling tool that provides insights into Java applications' performance by collecting and analysing data about CPU usage, memory allocation, and thread behaviour.

Eclipse Memory Analyzer (MAT): MAT is a memory analysis tool that helps identify memory leaks and optimize memory usage in Java applications. It allows developers to analyse heap dumps and provides visual representations of memory consumption.

# IntelliJ IDEA

## Introduction

IntelliJ IDEA is a popular integrated development environment (IDE) that offers a comprehensive set of tools and features for Java and other programming languages. It provides a user-friendly interface and powerful capabilities to streamline the software development process. In this article, we will walk you through the steps of writing and running a program in IntelliJ IDEA, helping you get started with this versatile IDE.

## Step 1: Installing IntelliJ IDEA

Before we begin, make sure you have IntelliJ IDEA installed on your system. You can download the Community Edition for free from the official JetBrains website ( https://www.jetbrains.com/idea/). Follow the installation instructions provided for your specific operating system.

## Step 2: Creating a New Project

Launch IntelliJ IDEA and click on "Create New Project" or go to "File" > "New" > "Project". Select the desired project type, such as Java, and configure the project settings like project name, location, and SDK (Software Development Kit) version. Click "Next" and follow the prompts to create the project.

## Step 3: Writing Your Program

Once your project is created, you will see the project structure on the left-hand side of the IDE. Right-click on the source folder (e.g., "src") and select "New" > "Java Class". Enter a class name for your program and click "OK". IntelliJ IDEA will generate a Java class file for you.

In the editor window, you can start writing your program code. Add the necessary statements, variables, and logic to achieve the desired functionality. IntelliJ IDEA provides helpful features like code completion, auto-formatting, and code analysis to assist you during the coding process.

## Step 4: Building the Project

After writing your program, you need to build the project to compile the code and generate the necessary artifacts. IntelliJ IDEA automatically compiles your code as you write, but you can also manually trigger the build process by selecting "Build" > "Build Project" from the menu or using the associated keyboard shortcut.

## Step 5: Running Your Program

To run your program, navigate to the class containing the main method (usually named "Main" or similar) that serves as the entry point for execution. Right-click inside the editor window and select "Run <class name>" or use the keyboard shortcut for running the program. IntelliJ IDEA will execute your program and display the output in the console window.

## Step 6: Debugging

IntelliJ IDEA offers powerful debugging capabilities to help you identify and fix issues in your code. You can set breakpoints by clicking on the left margin of the editor window or using the "Run" > "Toggle Line Breakpoint" option. Run your program in debug mode, and it will pause at the breakpoints, allowing you to inspect variables, step through the code, and analyse program flow.

## Step 7: Project Management

IntelliJ IDEA provides various project management features to organize your code effectively. You can create packages, add additional source files, manage external libraries, and configure build settings. Utilize the project view and navigation tools to navigate through your project's files and classes seamlessly.

# Revision

## Compiling and Running a Java Program

- Install Java Development Kit (JDK)
- Write Your Java Program
- Save Your Java Program
- Open a Terminal or Command Prompt
- Navigate to the Program Directory
- Compile Your Java Program
- Run Your Java Program

## Java Development Tools

### 1.Integrated Development Environments (IDEs)

- Eclipse
- IntelliJ IDEA
- NetBeans

### 2. Build Tools

- Apache Maven
- Gradle

### 3. Version Control Systems (VCS)

- Git
- Subversion (SVN)

### 4. Testing Frameworks

- JUnit
- TestNG

## 5. Profiling and Debugging Tools

- Java VisualVM
- Eclipse Memory Analyzer (MAT)

## IntelliJ IDE

- Installing IntelliJ IDEA
- Creating a New Project
- Writing Your Program
- Building the Project
- Running Your Program
- Debugging
- Project management

Section 9

# Progressions

# Ch 36

# Arithmetic Progression

## Introduction

Arithmetic Progression (AP) is a fundamental concept in mathematics that deals with a sequence of numbers in which the difference between any two consecutive terms remains constant. It is a widely studied topic with applications in various fields, including algebra, number theory, finance, and computer science. In this chapter, we will explore arithmetic progression in detail, covering its properties, common formulas, and real-world applications.

## What is Arithmetic Progression?

Arithmetic Progression, also known as arithmetic sequence, is a sequence of numbers in which the difference between consecutive terms remains constant. This constant difference is called the common difference (d). Each term in the sequence can be obtained by adding the common difference to the previous term. The general form of an arithmetic progression is: a, a + d, a + 2d, a + 3d..., where 'a' is the first term and 'd' is the common difference.

## Properties of Arithmetic Progression

1. Common Difference (d): The common difference is the fixed value by which each term differs from the previous term. It determines the pattern and direction of the sequence.
2. First Term (a): The first term of the arithmetic progression sets the starting point of the sequence.

3. Nth Term (a_n): The nth term of the arithmetic progression can be calculated using the formula: $a_n = a + (n-1) * d$, where 'a' is the first term and 'd' is the common difference.
4. Number of Terms (n): The number of terms in an arithmetic progression can be determined by various methods, such as using the formula: $n = ((a_n - a) / d) + 1$.

## Formulas for Arithmetic Progression

Nth Term (a_n): $a_n = a + (n-1) * d$

Sum of first N Terms (S_n): $S_n = (n/2) * (2a + (n-1) * d)$

## Applications of Arithmetic Progression

Arithmetic Progression finds applications in various fields, including:

Finance: AP is used in financial calculations, such as calculating compound interest, loan amortization, and investment growth over time.

Series and Sequences: AP plays a crucial role in the study of series and sequences, which have wide-ranging applications in mathematics and computer science.

Number Patterns: AP helps identify and analyse patterns in numbers, such as consecutive integers and consecutive prime numbers.

## Example

Let's consider an example to illustrate arithmetic progression:

Find the $10^{th}$ term of an arithmetic progression where the first term (a) is 2 and the common difference (d) is 4.

Using the formula for the nth term, we can calculate the $10^{th}$ term as follows:

a_10 = a + (n-1) * d

= 2 + (10-1) * 4

= 2 + 9 * 4 = 2 + 36 = 38

The $10^{th}$ term of the arithmetic progression is 38.

Ch 37

# Nth Term in an Arithmetic Progression

## Introduction

Arithmetic Progression (AP) is a sequence of numbers in which the difference between consecutive terms remains constant. One common task in AP is finding the Nth term, which allows us to determine the value of any term in the sequence. In this chapter, we will explore an iterative approach to finding the Nth term in an Arithmetic Progression. We will discuss the understanding, approach, step-by-step solution, and provide sample code to illustrate the process.

## Understanding Arithmetic Progression

Arithmetic Progression is a sequence of numbers in which the difference between consecutive terms, known as the common difference, remains constant. Each term can be obtained by adding the common difference to the previous term. The Nth term represents the value of the term at position N in the sequence.

## Approach

To find the Nth term in an Arithmetic Progression using iteration, we can start with the first term and repeatedly add the common difference until we reach the desired position N.

## Step-by-Step Solution

Input the first term (a), the common difference (d), and the position of the term we want to find (N).

Initialize a variable (currentTerm) to store the current term. Set it equal to the first term (a).

Iterate from 1 to N-1:

- Add the common difference (d) to the current term (currentTerm).
- Update the current term with the new value.
- After the loop, the currentTerm will hold the value of the Nth term in the Arithmetic Progression.
- Output the Nth term.

## Code

Here's an example implementation:

```java
import java.util.Scanner;

public class ArithmeticProgressionNthTerm {
    public static void main(String[] args) {
        Scanner scanner = new Scanner(System.in);

        System.out.print("Enter the first term (a): ");
        int firstTerm = scanner.nextInt();

        System.out.print("Enter the common difference (d): ");
        int commonDifference = scanner.nextInt();

        System.out.print("Enter the position of the term (N): ");
        int position = scanner.nextInt();

        int currentTerm = firstTerm;

        for (int i = 1; i < position; i++) {
            currentTerm += commonDifference;
        }

        System.out.println("The " + position + "th term in the Arithmetic Progression is: " + currentTerm);
    }
}
```

Ch 38

# Sum of Terms in an Arithmetic Progression

## Introduction

Arithmetic Progression (AP) is a sequence of numbers in which the difference between consecutive terms remains constant. One common task in AP is finding the sum of terms, which allows us to determine the total value of all terms in the sequence up to a certain position. In this chapter, we will explore an iterative approach to finding the sum of terms in an Arithmetic Progression. We will discuss the understanding, approach, step-by-step solution, and provide sample code to illustrate the process.

## Understanding Arithmetic Progression

Arithmetic Progression is a sequence of numbers in which the difference between consecutive terms, known as the common difference, remains constant. Each term can be obtained by adding the common difference to the previous term. The sum of terms represents the total value of all terms in the sequence up to a certain position.

## Approach

To find the sum of terms in an Arithmetic Progression using iteration, we can start with the first term and repeatedly add the terms up to the desired position.

## Step-by-Step Solution

1. Input the first term (a), the common difference (d), and the position of the last term (N) for which we want to find the sum.
2. Initialize a variable (sum) to store the sum of terms. Set it equal to the first term (a).
3. Initialize a variable (currentTerm) to store the current term. Set it equal to the first term (a).
4. Iterate from 2 to N:
   a. Add the common difference (d) to the current term (currentTerm).
   b. Add the current term to the sum of terms (sum).
5. After the loop, the sum will hold the total value of all terms in the Arithmetic Progression up to the position N.
6. Output the sum of terms.

## Code

Here's an example implementation:

```
import java.util.Scanner;

public class ArithmeticProgressionSum {
    public static void main(String[] args) {
        Scanner scanner = new Scanner(System.in);

        System.out.print("Enter the first term (a): ");
        int firstTerm = scanner.nextInt();

        System.out.print("Enter the common difference (d): ");
        int commonDifference = scanner.nextInt();

        System.out.print("Enter the position of the last term (N): ");
        int lastTermPosition = scanner.nextInt();

        int sum = firstTerm;
        int currentTerm = firstTerm;

        for (int i = 2; i <= lastTermPosition; i++) {
            currentTerm += commonDifference;
            sum += currentTerm;
        }

        System.out.println("The sum of terms in the Arithmetic Progression is: " + sum);
    }
}
```

# Geometric Progression

## Introduction

Geometric Progression (GP) is a fundamental concept in mathematics that involves a sequence of numbers in which each term is obtained by multiplying the previous term by a fixed, non-zero value called the common ratio. Geometric Progression finds applications in a wide range of fields, including algebra, finance, physics, and computer science. In this chapter, we will explore the intricacies of geometric progression, unravelling its properties, formulas, and practical applications.

## Understanding Geometric Progression

Geometric Progression is a sequence of numbers in which the ratio between any two consecutive terms remains constant. This constant ratio is denoted by 'r' and defines the pattern and behaviour of the progression. The terms in a geometric progression can be represented using the general formula: $a_n = a_1 * r^{(n-1)}$, where 'a_n' represents the nth term, 'a_1' denotes the first term, 'n' represents the position of the term, and 'r' is the common ratio.

## Properties of Geometric Progression

Common Ratio (r): The common ratio is the fixed value by which each term in the geometric progression is multiplied to obtain the next term. It determines the pattern and direction of the progression.

First Term ($a_1$): The first term, denoted by '$a_1$', is the starting point of the geometric progression. It sets the initial value from which subsequent terms are derived.

Nth Term ($a_n$): The nth term of the geometric progression, represented by '$a_n$', is calculated using the formula: $a_n = a_1 * r^{(n-1)}$

Number of Terms (n): The number of terms in a geometric progression can be calculated using the formula: $n = \log_r (a_n / a_1) + 1$

Sum of Terms ($S_n$): The sum of the first 'n' terms of a geometric progression can be calculated using the formula: $S_n = a_1 * (r^n - 1)/ (r - 1)$

## Applications of Geometric Progression

Geometric Progression finds applications in various real-world scenarios, including:

Financial Growth: GP is used to model compound interest, investment growth, and exponential decay in financial calculations.

Physics and Science: Geometric Progression is employed to describe exponential growth and decay phenomena, such as radioactive decay and population growth.

Computer Science: GP plays a role in algorithms, data structures, and optimization problems that involve exponential time complexity or growth.

## Example

Let's consider an example to illustrate geometric progression:

Find the sum of the first 5 terms of a geometric progression where the first term ($a_1$) is 2 and the common ratio (r) is 3.

Using the formula for the sum of terms, $S_n = a_1 * (r^n - 1) / (r - 1)$, we can calculate the sum as follows:

$S_5 = 2 * ((3^5 - 1) / (3 - 1))$

$= 2 * ((243 - 1) / 2)$

$= 2 * (242 / 2)$

$= 2 * 121$

$= 242$

The sum of the first 5 terms of the geometric progression is 242.

Ch 40

# Nth Term in a Geometric Progression

## Introduction

Geometric Progression (GP) is a sequence of numbers in which each term is obtained by multiplying the previous term by a constant ratio. In this chapter, we will discuss an iterative approach to finding the Nth term in a Geometric Progression. We will cover the understanding of Geometric Progression, the approach to finding the Nth term, and provide a step-by-step solution with sample code.

## Understanding Geometric Progression

A Geometric Progression is a sequence of numbers in which each term, starting from the second term, is obtained by multiplying the previous term by a fixed ratio called the common ratio (r). The general form of a Geometric Progression is a, ar, $ar^2$, $ar^3$..., where 'a' is the first term and 'r' is the common ratio.

## Approach

To find the Nth term in a Geometric Progression, we can use an iterative approach. Starting from the first term (a), we can multiply the term by the common ratio (r), N-1 times to obtain the Nth term. By iteratively applying the common ratio, we can calculate the desired term efficiently.

## Step-by-Step Solution

1. Input the values of the first term 'a', the common ratio 'r', and the value of N representing the term we want to find.
2. Initialize a variable 'currentTerm' with the value of the first term 'a'.
3. Iterate N-1 times:

   a. Multiply the 'currentTerm' by the common ratio 'r'.

   b. Update the value of 'currentTerm' with the result of the multiplication.

4. The value of 'currentTerm' after the loop will be the Nth term in the Geometric Progression.

## Code

Here's an example implementation for finding the Nth term in a Geometric Progression using iteration:

```
import java.util.*;

public class GeometricProgression {
    public static void main(String[] args) {
        Scanner scanner = new Scanner(System.in);

        System.out.print("Enter the first term (a): ");
        double a = scanner.nextDouble();

        System.out.print("Enter the common ratio (r): ");
        double r = scanner.nextDouble();

        System.out.print("Enter the value of N: ");
        int N = scanner.nextInt();

        double currentTerm = a;
        for (int i = 1; i < N; i++) {
            currentTerm *= r;
        }

        System.out.println("The " + N + "th term in the Geometric Progression is: " + currentTerm);
    }
}
```

# Ch 41

## Sum of Terms in a Geometric Progression

### Introduction

Geometric Progression (GP) is a sequence of numbers in which each term is obtained by multiplying the previous term by a constant ratio. In this article, we will discuss an iterative approach to finding the sum of terms in a Geometric Progression. We will cover the understanding of Geometric Progression, the approach to finding the sum of terms, and provide a step-by-step solution with sample code.

### Approach

To find the sum of terms in a Geometric Progression, we can use an iterative approach. Starting from the first term (a), we can multiply the term by the common ratio (r) and sum up the terms for the desired number of iterations. By iteratively applying the common ratio and accumulating the terms, we can calculate the sum efficiently.

### Step-by-Step Solution

Input the values of the first term 'a', the common ratio 'r', and the number of terms 'n' for which we want to find the sum.

Initialize a variable 'sum' to 0.

Iterate 'n' times: a. Multiply the first term 'a' by the common ratio 'r' raised to the power of the current iteration. b. Add the result to the 'sum' variable.

The value of 'sum' after the loop will be the sum of terms in the Geometric Progression.

## Code

Here's an example implementation in Java for finding the sum of terms in a Geometric Progression using iteration:

```
import java.util.*;

public class GeometricProgressionSum {
    public static void main(String[] args) {
        Scanner scanner = new Scanner(System.in);

        System.out.print("Enter the first term (a): ");
        double a = scanner.nextDouble();

        System.out.print("Enter the common ratio (r): ");
        double r = scanner.nextDouble();

        System.out.print("Enter the number of terms (n): ");
        int n = scanner.nextInt();

        double sum = 0;
        double term = a;

        for (int i = 0; i < n; i++) {
            sum += term;
            term *= r;
        }

        System.out.println("The sum of " + n + " terms in the Geometric Progression is: " + sum);
    }
}
```

## Revision

### What is Arithmetic Progression

Arithmetic Progression, also known as arithmetic sequence, is a sequence of numbers in which the difference between consecutive terms remains constant. This constant difference is called the common difference (d). Each term in the sequence can be obtained by adding the common difference to the previous term. The general form of an arithmetic progression is: a, a + d, a + 2d, a + 3d..., where 'a' is the first term and 'd' is the common difference.

### Nth Term in an AP

Nth term in an AP can be calculated using

1. Formula: (a_n): a_n = a + (n-1) * d
2. Keep on adding common difference(d) to the first term

## Code

```
import java.util.Scanner;

public class ArithmeticProgressionNthTerm {
    public static void main(String[] args) {
        Scanner scanner = new Scanner(System.in);

        System.out.print("Enter the first term (a): ");
        int firstTerm = scanner.nextInt();

        System.out.print("Enter the common difference (d): ");
        int commonDifference = scanner.nextInt();

        System.out.print("Enter the position of the term (N): ");
        int position = scanner.nextInt();

        int currentTerm = firstTerm;

        for (int i = 1; i < position; i++) {
            currentTerm += commonDifference;
        }

        System.out.println("The " + position + "th term in the Arithmetic Progression is: " + currentTerm);
    }
}
```

## Sum of n Terms in an AP

Sum of n terms in an AP can be calculated using

1. Formula: (S_n): S_n = (n/2) * (2a + (n-1) * d)
2. Keep on adding the current term to the sum

## Code

```
import java.util.Scanner;

public class ArithmeticProgressionSum {
    public static void main(String[] args) {
        Scanner scanner = new Scanner(System.in);

        System.out.print("Enter the first term (a): ");
        int firstTerm = scanner.nextInt();

        System.out.print("Enter the common difference (d): ");
        int commonDifference = scanner.nextInt();

        System.out.print("Enter the position of the last term (N): ");
        int lastTermPosition = scanner.nextInt();

        int sum = firstTerm;
        int currentTerm = firstTerm;

        for (int i = 2; i <= lastTermPosition; i++) {
            currentTerm += commonDifference;
            sum += currentTerm;
        }

        System.out.println("The sum of terms in the Arithmetic Progression is: " + sum);
    }
}
```

## What is Geometric Progression

Geometric Progression is a sequence of numbers in which the ratio between any two consecutive terms remains constant. This constant ratio is denoted by 'r' and defines the pattern and behaviour of the progression. The terms in a geometric progression can be represented using the general formula: a_n = a_1 * $r^{(n-1)}$, where 'a_n' represents the nth term, 'a_1' denotes the first term, 'n' represents the position of the term, and 'r' is the common ratio.

## Nth Term in a GP

Nth term in an GP can be calculated using

1. Formula: $a\_n = a\_1 * r^{(n-1)}$
2. Keep on multiplying common ratio(r) to the first term

## Code

```
import java.util.*;

public class GeometricProgression {
    public static void main(String[] args) {
        Scanner scanner = new Scanner(System.in);

        System.out.print("Enter the first term (a): ");
        double a = scanner.nextDouble();

        System.out.print("Enter the common ratio (r): ");
        double r = scanner.nextDouble();

        System.out.print("Enter the value of N: ");
        int N = scanner.nextInt();

        double currentTerm = a;
        for (int i = 1; i < N; i++) {
            currentTerm *= r;
        }

        System.out.println("The " + N + "th term in the Geometric Progression is: " + currentTerm);
    }
}
```

## Sum of n Terms in a GP

Sum of n terms in an GP can be calculated using

1. Formula: $a\_1 * ((r^n - 1) / (r - 1))$
2. Keep on adding the current term to the sum

## ➢ Sum of Terms in a Geometric Progression ➣

**Code**

```
import java.util.*;

public class GeometricProgressionSum {
    public static void main(String[] args) {
        Scanner scanner = new Scanner(System.in);

        System.out.print("Enter the first term (a): ");
        double a = scanner.nextDouble();

        System.out.print("Enter the common ratio (r): ");
        double r = scanner.nextDouble();

        System.out.print("Enter the number of terms (n): ");
        int n = scanner.nextInt();

        double sum = 0;
        double term = a;

        for (int i = 0; i < n; i++) {
            sum += term;
            term *= r;
        }

        System.out.println("The sum of " + n + " terms in the Geometric Progression is: " + sum);
    }
}
```

## Section 10

# Math Problems

# Area of a Circle

## Introduction

Calculating the area of a circle is a fundamental mathematical operation. In this chapter, we will discuss an iterative approach to finding the area of a circle. We will cover the understanding of the circle's properties, the approach to finding the area, and provide a step-by-step solution with sample code.

## Understanding the Circle

A circle is a geometric shape consisting of all points in a plane that are equidistant from a fixed centre point. The distance from the centre point to any point on the circle is called the radius (r), and the ratio of the circumference of the circle to its diameter is represented by the mathematical constant pi (π).

## Approach

To find the area of a circle, we can use the formula $A = \pi * r^2$, where A represents the area and r is the radius of the circle. By squaring the radius and multiplying it by the value of π, we can calculate the area of the circle iteratively.

**Step-by-Step Solution**

1. Input the value of the radius 'r' of the circle.
2. Define a constant variable 'pi' with the value of 3.14159 (or use the built-in constant Math.PI in programming languages like Java).

3. Calculate the area of the circle using the formula A = pi * $r^2$.
4. The calculated value of 'A' will be the area of the circle.

## Code

Here's an example implementation for finding the area of a circle using iteration:

```
import java.util.*;

public class CircleArea {
    public static void main(String[] args) {
        Scanner scanner = new Scanner(System.in);

        System.out.print("Enter the radius of the circle: ");
        double radius = scanner.nextDouble();

        double pi = Math.PI;
        double area = pi * Math.pow(radius, 2);

        System.out.println("The area of the circle is: " + area);
    }
}
```

# Finding GCD Using Euclid's Algo

## Introduction

Euclid's algorithm is a method for finding the greatest common divisor (GCD) of two integers. The GCD is the largest positive integer that divides both numbers without leaving a remainder. In this chapter, we will discuss the understanding of Euclid's algorithm, the approach to finding the GCD, and provide a step-by-step solution with sample code.

## Understanding Euclid's Algorithm

Euclid's algorithm is based on the principle that the GCD of two numbers remains the same if the larger number is replaced by the difference between the larger and smaller numbers. The algorithm repeatedly applies this principle until the remainder becomes zero, at which point the smaller number becomes the GCD.

## Approach

To find the GCD of two numbers using Euclid's algorithm, we start with two positive integers 'a' and 'b'. We repeatedly divide the larger number by the smaller number and update the numbers until the remainder becomes zero. The last non-zero remainder is the GCD of the original two numbers.

## Step-by-Step Solution

1. Input the two positive integers 'a' and 'b' for which we want to find the GCD.
2. Initialize two variables, 'x' and 'y', with the values of 'a' and 'b', respectively.
3. While 'y' is not equal to zero:
    a. Set 'temp' equal to the value of 'y'.
    b. Set 'y' equal to the remainder when 'x' is divided by 'y'.
    c. Set 'x' equal to the value of 'temp'.
4. The value of 'x' after the loop will be the GCD of 'a' and 'b'.

## Code

Here's an example implementation for finding the GCD of two numbers using Euclid's algorithm:

```
public class EuclidsAlgorithm {
    public static void main(String[] args) {
        Scanner scanner = new Scanner(System.in);

        System.out.print("Enter the first number: ");
        int a = scanner.nextInt();

        System.out.print("Enter the second number: ");
        int b = scanner.nextInt();

        int x = a;
        int y = b;

        while (y != 0) {
            int temp = y;
            y = x % y;
            x = temp;
        }

        System.out.println("The GCD of " + a + " and " + b + " is: " + x);
    }
}
```

# Ch 44

# Functions in Java

## Introduction

Functions, also known as methods, play a vital role in programming. They allow us to break down complex tasks into smaller, manageable parts, making our code more organized, reusable, and easier to maintain. In this chapter, we will explore the concept of functions, understand their importance, and learn how to create and use functions effectively.

## Understanding Functions in Java

A function is a block of code that performs a specific task. It can take inputs, called parameters, and optionally return a value. Functions encapsulate a set of operations, allowing us to modularize our code and achieve better code readability, reusability, and maintainability.

## Approach

To work with functions in Java, we follow these key steps:

1. Function Declaration: Specify the return type, function name, and parameter list (if any) of the function.
2. Function Definition: Implement the functionality of the function within its block of code.
3. Function Invocation: Call or invoke the function from other parts of the program, providing the necessary arguments.

## Step-by-Step Solution

1. Function Declaration
   a. Determine the purpose of the function and its return type.
   b. Choose a descriptive function name that reflects its functionality.
   c. Define the parameters the function requires, specifying their types and names.
2. Function Definition
   a. Begin the function body by specifying the return type (void if no return value).
   b. Implement the desired functionality using statements and control flow structures.
   c. If applicable, use the return keyword to return a value of the specified return type.
3. Function Invocation
   a. Identify the location in the code where the function should be called.
   b. Provide arguments that match the function's parameter list, if any.

## Code

Here's an example implementation to illustrate the concept of functions:

```
import java.util.*;


public class FunctionsExample {

    // Function declaration
    public static int addNumbers(int a, int b) {
        int sum = a + b;
        return sum;
    }

    public static void main(String[] args) {
        // Function invocation
        int result = addNumbers(5, 7);
        System.out.println("The sum is: " + result);
    }
}
```

# Number Systems

## Introduction

In the world of digital computing and mathematics, different number systems are used to represent and manipulate numbers. The two most fundamental number systems are the Decimal Number System and the Binary Number System. In this chapter, we will explore these number systems, understand their concepts, discuss their representations, and highlight their significance in various domains.

## Decimal Number System

The Decimal Number System, also known as the Base-10 system, is the number system most commonly used by humans. It is called "decimal" because it utilizes ten distinct symbols or digits: 0, 1, 2, 3, 4, 5, 6, 7, 8, and 9. Each digit's positional value is based on powers of 10. The rightmost digit represents the units place, the next digit represents the tens place, and so on.

For example, the number 537 in the decimal system represents (5 x 10^2) + (3 x 10^1) + (7 x 10^0) = 500 + 30 + 7 = 537.

## Binary Number System

The Binary Number System, also known as the Base-2 system, is a fundamental number system in computer science and digital electronics. It consists of only two digits: 0 and 1. Each digit's positional value is based on powers of 2. The rightmost digit represents the units place ($2^0$), the next digit represents the twos place ($2^1$), the following digit represents the fours place ($2^2$), and so on.

For example, the binary number 101 represents $(1 \times 2^2) + (0 \times 2^1) + (1 \times 2^0) = 4 + 0 + 1 = 5$ in the decimal system.

## Comparison and Conversion

The decimal and binary number systems have distinct characteristics and are used in different contexts. The decimal system is intuitive for human comprehension and is widely used in everyday life, including mathematics, finance, and general counting. On the other hand, the binary system is fundamental to computer systems, where information is represented using binary digits (bits).

Converting a decimal number to binary involves dividing the decimal number successively by 2 and recording the remainders in reverse order. The process is repeated until the quotient becomes zero. For example, the decimal number 14 in binary is 1110.

Converting a binary number to decimal involves multiplying each binary digit by the corresponding power of 2 and summing the results. For example, the binary number 1101 in decimal is $(1 \times 2^3) + (1 \times 2^2) + (0 \times 2^1) + (1 \times 2^0) = 13$.

## Applications and Significance

The Decimal and Binary Number Systems play vital roles in various fields:

### Computing

Binary numbers are fundamental to computer systems, where data is processed, stored, and transmitted in binary format. Binary representations enable efficient computation and logical operations in digital circuits.

### Data Storage

Binary representations are used to store information in computer memory, hard drives, and other digital storage devices. Each bit represents the presence or absence of electrical charge, forming the basis for digital data storage.

### Networking and Communication

Binary data transmission is the backbone of computer networks and communication protocols. Binary encoding allows reliable and efficient transfer of data across different systems.

### Cryptography

Binary numbers are essential in encryption algorithms and cryptographic systems, providing secure communication and data protection.

# Converting Decimal to Binary

## Introduction

Converting decimal numbers to binary is a fundamental operation in computer science and digital systems. The binary number system, consisting of 0s and 1s, is widely used in computing and represents the foundation of digital data representation.

## Approach

To convert a decimal number to binary, we can follow the following approach:

1. Start with the given decimal number.
2. Divide the decimal number by 2.
3. Record the remainder (0 or 1).
4. Repeat steps 2 and 3 with the quotient obtained from the previous division until the quotient becomes zero.
5. Concatenate the remainders obtained in reverse order to obtain the binary representation.

**Step-by-Step Solution**

Let's illustrate the conversion process using an example:

## Example

Convert the decimal number 42 to binary.

Step 1: Start with the decimal number 42.

Step 2: Divide 42 by 2. The quotient is 21, and the remainder is 0.

Step 3: Divide 21 by 2. The quotient is 10, and the remainder is 1.

Step 4: Divide 10 by 2. The quotient is 5, and the remainder is 0.

Step 5: Divide 5 by 2. The quotient is 2, and the remainder is 1.

Step 6: Divide 2 by 2. The quotient is 1, and the remainder is 0.

Step 7: Divide 1 by 2. The quotient is 0, and the remainder is 1.

Recording the remainders in reverse order, we obtain the binary representation: 101010.

## Code

Here's an example implementation for converting a decimal number to binary:

```
public class DecimalToBinary {
  public static void main(String[] args) {
      int decimalNumber = 42;
      StringBuilder binaryNumber = new StringBuilder();

      while (decimalNumber > 0) {
          int remainder = decimalNumber % 2;
          binaryNumber.insert(0, remainder);
          decimalNumber /= 2;
      }

      System.out.println("Binary representation: " + binaryNumber);
  }
}
```

## Output

Binary representation: 101010

# Converting Binary to Decimal

## Introduction

Converting binary numbers to decimal is a fundamental process in computer science and digital systems. The binary number system, composed of 0s and 1s, is extensively used in computing and serves as the foundation for digital data representation. In this chapter, we will explore the concept of binary to decimal conversion, provide an understanding of the process, discuss the approach to conversion, present a step-by-step solution, and provide a code example.

## Approach

To convert a binary number to decimal, we can follow the following approach:

1. Start with the given binary number.
2. Begin from the rightmost digit (units place).
3. Multiply each binary digit by the corresponding power of 2 based on its position.
4. Sum up the products obtained in step 3 to get the decimal representation.

**Step-by-Step Solution**

Let's illustrate the conversion process using an example:

**Example**

Convert the binary number 101010 to decimal.

Step 1: Start with the binary number 101010.

Step 2: Begin from the rightmost digit (0) and assign a position value of $2^0$ (units place).

Step 3: Multiply the rightmost digit (0) by the corresponding power of 2 ($2^0$), resulting in 0.

Step 4: Move to the next digit (1) and assign a position value of $2^1$ (twos place).

Step 5: Multiply the digit (1) by the corresponding power of 2 ($2^1$), resulting in 2.

Step 6: Repeat steps 4 and 5 for each subsequent digit, assigning increasing powers of 2.

Step 7: Sum up the products obtained in step 5: 0 + 2 + 0 + 8 + 0 + 32 = 42.

Therefore, the binary number 101010 is equivalent to the decimal number 42.

## Code

Here's an example implementation for converting a binary number to decimal:

```
public class BinaryToDecimal {
  public static void main(String[] args) {
      String binaryNumber = "101010";
      int decimalNumber = 0;
      int power = 0;

      for (int i = binaryNumber.length() - 1; i >= 0; i--) {
          int digit = Character.getNumericValue(binaryNumber.charAt(i));
          decimalNumber += digit * Math.pow(2, power);
          power++;
      }

      System.out.println("Decimal representation: " + decimalNumber);
  }
}
```

Output

Decimal representation: 42

Ch 48

# Understanding the Modulo Operator

The modulo operator, often represented by the symbol %, is a fundamental mathematical operation that is widely used in programming. It returns the remainder of a division operation. This operator is particularly useful in various scenarios such as checking for even/odd numbers, cycling through a set of values, or ensuring values wrap around within a certain range.

## What is the Modulo Operator?

In simple terms, the modulo operation finds the remainder after division of one number by another. For example, 7 % 3 yields 1 because 7 divided by 3 is 2 with a remainder of 1.

## Syntax

```
int result = a % b;
```

Here, a is divided by b, and the remainder is stored in result.

## Use Cases of Modulo Operator

1. **Checking for Even/Odd Numbers**
    - A number is even if it is divisible by 2 (num % 2 == 0).
    - A number is odd if it is not divisible by 2 (num % 2 != 0).

2. **Cyclic Operations**

The modulo operator can be used to cycle through a set of values. For example, in a circular buffer or to ensure array indices wrap around.

3. **Date Calculations**

It helps in calculating weeks, days, months, and other date-related operations where remainders are essential.

## Approach to Using the Modulo Operator

To understand and effectively use the modulo operator, follow these steps:

1. **Identify the Need**

Determine where you need to use the modulo operation. For instance, finding remainders, checking for divisibility, or cyclic iterations.

2. **Apply the Operator**

Use the % operator with the appropriate operands. Ensure the divisor is not zero, as division by zero is undefined and will throw an exception.

3. **Interpret the Result**

Analyse the result to implement the desired logic, whether it's for condition checks, looping constructs, or other logical operations.

## Example: Checking Even or Odd

### Problem

Check if a number is even or odd using the modulo operator.

### Approach

1. Read the input number.
2. Use the modulo operator to determine if the number is divisible by 2.
3. Print whether the number is even or odd.

### Code

```
import java.util.Scanner;

public class EvenOddChecker {
    public static void main(String[] args) {
        Scanner scanner = new Scanner(System.in);
        System.out.print("Enter a number: ");
        int num = scanner.nextInt();

        if (num % 2 == 0) {
            System.out.println(num + " is even.");
        } else {
            System.out.println(num + " is odd.");
        }
    }
}
```

## Revision

### Area of Circle

1. Input the value of the radius 'r' of the circle.
2. Define a constant variable 'pi' with the value of 3.14159 (or use the built-in constant Math.PI in programming languages like Java).
3. Calculate the area of the circle using the formula $A = pi * r^2$.
4. The calculated value of 'A' will be the area of the circle.

### Finding GCD using Euclid's algo

1. Input the two positive integers 'a' and 'b' for which we want to find the GCD.
2. Initialize two variables, 'x' and 'y', with the values of 'a' and 'b', respectively.
3. While 'y' is not equal to zero:
    - Set 'temp' equal to the value of 'y'.
    - Set 'y' equal to the remainder when 'x' is divided by 'y'.
    - Set 'x' equal to the value of 'temp'.
4. The value of 'x' after the loop will be the GCD of 'a' and 'b'.

### Functions in Java

1. Function Declaration
    - Determine the purpose of the function and its return type.
    - Choose a descriptive function name that reflects its functionality.

- Define the parameters the function requires, specifying their types and names.

2. Function Definition

- Begin the function body by specifying the return type (void if no return value).
- Implement the desired functionality using statements and control flow structures.
- If applicable, use the return keyword to return a value of the specified return type.

3. Function Invocation

- Identify the location in the code where the function should be called.
- Provide arguments that match the function's parameter list, if any.

## Number Systems

### 1. Decimal Number System

The Decimal Number System, also known as the Base-10 system, is the number system most commonly used by humans. It is called "decimal" because it utilizes ten distinct symbols or digits: 0, 1, 2, 3, 4, 5, 6, 7, 8, and 9. Each digit's positional value is based on powers of 10. The rightmost digit represents the units place, the next digit represents the tens place, and so on.

For example, the number 537 in the decimal system represents (5 x 10^2) + (3 x 10^1) + (7 x 10^0) = 500 + 30 + 7 = 537.

## 2. Binary Number System

The Binary Number System, also known as the Base-2 system, is a fundamental number system in computer science and digital electronics. It consists of only two digits: 0 and 1. Each digit's positional value is based on powers of 2. The rightmost digit represents the units place (2^0), the next digit represents the twos place (2^1), the following digit represents the fours place (2^2), and so on.

For example, the binary number 101 represents (1 x 2^2) + (0 x 2^1) + (1 x 2^0) = 4 + 0 + 1 = 5 in the decimal system.

## 3. Decimal to Binary

```
public class DecimalToBinary {
  public static void main(String[] args) {
      int decimalNumber = 42;
      StringBuilder binaryNumber = new StringBuilder();

      while (decimalNumber > 0) {
          int remainder = decimalNumber % 2;
          binaryNumber.insert(0, remainder);
          decimalNumber /= 2;
      }

      System.out.println("Binary representation: " + binaryNumber);
  }
}
```

4. Binary to Decimal

```
public class BinaryToDecimal {
  public static void main(String[] args) {
      String binaryNumber = "101010";
      int decimalNumber = 0;
      int power = 0;

      for (int i = binaryNumber.length() - 1; i >= 0; i--) {
          int digit = Character.getNumericValue(binaryNumber.charAt(i));
          decimalNumber += digit * Math.pow(2, power);
          power++;
      }

      System.out.println("Decimal representation: " + decimalNumber);
  }
}
```

## Modulo Operator

In simple terms, the modulo operation finds the remainder after division of one number by another. This operator is particularly useful in various scenarios such as checking for even/odd numbers.

## Example: Checking Even or Odd

### Problem

Check if a number is even or odd using the modulo operator.

### Approach

1. Read the input number.
2. Use the modulo operator to determine if the number is divisible by 2.
3. Print whether the number is even or odd.

```java
import java.util.Scanner;

public class EvenOddChecker {
    public static void main(String[] args) {
        Scanner scanner = new Scanner(System.in);
        System.out.print("Enter a number: ");
        int num = scanner.nextInt();

        if (num % 2 == 0) {
            System.out.println(num + " is even.");
        } else {
            System.out.println(num + " is odd.");
        }
    }
}
```

# Section 11

# Pattern Printing

# How to Solve Pattern Problems

## Introduction

Pattern problems are a common type of programming exercise that help improve your problem-solving skills and logical thinking. These problems involve creating specific shapes, numbers, or characters using loops and conditional statements. In this chapter, we will guide you through the process of solving pattern problems, providing step-by-step explanations and example solutions to help you master this skill.

## Understanding Pattern Problems

Pattern problems require you to print a specific arrangement of symbols, numbers, or characters in a structured manner. The patterns can vary in complexity, from simple geometric shapes to intricate designs. Solving pattern problems involves using loops (such as for, while, or do-while) and conditional statements to control the repetition and positioning of the elements in the pattern.

## Approach

To solve pattern problems effectively, it's important to follow a systematic approach. Here are the general steps you can take:

### 1. Analyse the Pattern

Carefully examine the given pattern and identify any repeating elements, sequences, or rules that govern the arrangement.

2. **Determine the Pattern Size**

Determine the size or number of rows and columns required to create the pattern. This will help you define the loop limits and control the iterations.

3. **Choose an Appropriate Loop**

Decide which loop construct (for, while, or do-while) is best suited for the pattern problem. Consider the pattern's structure and the conditions under which you need to repeat or terminate the loop.

4. **Implement the Logic**

Develop the logic to print the pattern using loops and conditional statements. Break down the pattern into smaller components and build the logic to generate each component iteratively.

5. **Test and Refine**

Test your solution by running it and verifying that the pattern is generated correctly. If the output doesn't match the expected pattern, review your code and make any necessary adjustments or corrections.

### Step-by-Step Solution with Example

Let's illustrate the approach with an example. Consider the following pattern problem:

**Pattern to Print**

```
1
22
333
4444
55555
```

## Solution

### 1. Analyse the Pattern

In this pattern, the number of rows corresponds to the value being printed, and each row contains a repetition of that number.

### 2. Determine the Pattern Size

The pattern has 5 rows.

### 3. Choose an Appropriate Loop

We will use a for loop to iterate from 1 to the desired number of rows (5 in this case).

### 4. Implement the Logic

Inside the loop, we will have an inner loop that repeats the current row number. We print the row number using the print() function, followed by a line break after each row.

```
int rows = 5;
for (int i = 1; i <= rows; i++) {
    for (int j = 1; j <= i; j++) {
        System.out.print(i);
    }
    System.out.println();
}
```

### 5. Test and Refine

When we run this code, it will print the desired pattern:

```
1
22
333
4444
55555
```

# Printing Left Half Pyramid of Stars

## Introduction

Creating patterns with stars is a common exercise in programming. In this chapter, we will focus on printing a left half pyramid of stars using java. We will discuss the understanding of the pattern, the approach to constructing it, and provide a step-by-step solution with sample code.

## Understanding the Left Half Pyramid of Stars

A left half pyramid is a pattern that consists of rows of stars, where each row contains one more star than the previous row. The stars are aligned to the right, forming a half pyramid-like shape.

## Approach

To print a left half pyramid of stars, we can follow the following approach:

1. Determine the number of rows in the pattern based on the desired size.
2. Use nested loops to iterate through the rows and columns.
3. Print the desired number of spaces followed by stars in each row, aligning them to the left.

## Step-by-Step Solution

1. Input the desired number of rows for the left half pyramid pattern.
2. Use a loop to iterate through each row from 1 to the desired number of rows:

    a. Use another loop to print the spaces before the stars.
    b. Print the desired number of spaces.
    c. Use another loop to print the stars.
    d. Print a star for each column up to the current row number.

3. After printing all the rows, the left half pyramid pattern will be displayed.

## Code

Here's an example implementation for printing a left half pyramid of stars:

```
import java.util.*;

public class LeftHalfPyramid {
    public static void main(String[] args) {
        Scanner scanner = new Scanner(System.in);

        System.out.print("Enter the number of rows: ");
        int numRows = scanner.nextInt();
        System.out.println();
        for (int row = 1; row <= numRows; row++) {
            for (int space = 1; space <= numRows - row; space++) {
                System.out.print("  ");
            }
            for (int star = 1; star <= row; star++) {
                System.out.print("* ");
            }
            System.out.println();
        }
    }
}
```

## Example Output

For numRows = 5, the output will be:

```
        *
      * *
    * * *
  * * * *
* * * * *
```

# Ch 51

# Printing Full Pyramid of Stars

## Introduction

Creating patterns with stars is a common exercise in programming. In this article, we will focus on printing a full pyramid of stars using java. We will discuss the understanding of the pattern, the approach to constructing it, and provide a step-by-step solution with sample code.

## Understanding the Full Pyramid of Stars

A full pyramid is a pattern that consists of rows of stars, where each row contains a gradually increasing number of stars. The stars are centred, forming a pyramid-like shape.

## Approach

To print a full pyramid of stars, we can follow the following approach

1. Determine the number of rows in the pattern based on the desired size.
2. Use nested loops to iterate through the rows and columns.
3. Print the desired number of spaces followed by stars in each row, aligning them to the centre.

**Step-by-Step Solution**

1. Input the desired number of rows for the full pyramid pattern.

2. Use a loop to iterate through each row from 1 to the desired number of rows:
   - Use another loop to print the spaces before the stars.
   - Print the desired number of spaces.
   - Use another loop to print the stars.
   - Print a star for each column up to the current row number, followed by another star for the next column.
3. After printing all the rows, the full pyramid pattern will be displayed.

**Code**

Here's an example implementation for printing a full pyramid of stars:

```
import java.util.*;
public class FullPyramid {
    public static void main(String[] args) {
        Scanner scanner = new Scanner(System.in);

        System.out.print("Enter the number of rows: ");
        int numRows = scanner.nextInt();
            System.out.println();
        int spaces = numRows - 1;

        for (int row = 1; row <= numRows; row++) {
            for (int space = 1; space <= spaces; space++) {
                System.out.print(" ");
            }
            spaces--;

            for (int star = 1; star <= 2 * row - 1; star++) {
                System.out.print("*");
            }
            System.out.println();
        }
    }
}
```

## Example Output

For numRows = 5, the output will be:

```
    *
   ***
  *****
 *******
*********
```

Ch 52

# Printing Inverted Right Half Pyramid of Stars

## Introduction

Creating patterns with stars is a common exercise in programming. In this article, we will focus on printing an inverted right half pyramid of stars using java. We will discuss the understanding of the pattern, the approach to constructing it, and provide a step-by-step solution with sample code.

## Understanding the Inverted Right Half Pyramid of Stars

An inverted right half pyramid is a pattern that consists of rows of stars, where each row contains a decreasing number of stars aligned to the right. The stars form an upside-down triangle shape.

## Approach

To print an inverted right half pyramid of stars, we can follow the following approach:

1. Determine the number of rows in the pattern based on the desired size.
2. Use nested loops to iterate through the rows and columns.
3. Print the desired number of stars in each row, aligned to the right.

Step-by-Step Solution

1. Input the desired number of rows for the inverted right half pyramid pattern.
2. Use a loop to iterate through each row from the desired number of rows to 1:
   - Use another loop to print the stars in each row.
   - Print a star for each column up to the current row number.
3. After printing all the rows, the inverted right half pyramid pattern will be displayed.

## Code

Here's an example implementation for printing an inverted right half pyramid of stars:

```
import java.util.*;

public class InvertedRightHalfPyramid {
    public static void main(String[] args) {
        Scanner scanner = new Scanner(System.in);

        System.out.print("Enter the number of rows: ");
        int numRows = scanner.nextInt();
            System.out.println();
        for (int row = numRows; row >= 1; row--) {
            for (int star = 1; star <= row; star++) {
                System.out.print("*");
            }
            System.out.println();
        }
    }
}
```

## Example Output

For numRows = 5, the output will be:

```
*****
****
***
**
*
```

# Revision

## Pattern Problem

1. Analyse the Pattern
2. Determine the Pattern Size
3. Choose an Appropriate Loop
4. Implement the Logic
5. Implement the Logic

## Left Half Pyramid

```
import java.util.*;

public class LeftHalfPyramid {
    public static void main(String[] args) {
        Scanner scanner = new Scanner(System.in);

        System.out.print("Enter the number of rows: ");
        int numRows = scanner.nextInt();
        System.out.println();
        for (int row = 1; row <= numRows; row++) {
            for (int space = 1; space <= numRows - row; space++) {
                System.out.print("  ");
            }
            for (int star = 1; star <= row; star++) {
                System.out.print("* ");
            }
            System.out.println();
        }
    }
}
```

Full Pyramid

```
import java.util.*;
public class FullPyramid {
    public static void main(String[] args) {
        Scanner scanner = new Scanner(System.in);

        System.out.print("Enter the number of rows: ");
        int numRows = scanner.nextInt();
            System.out.println();
        int spaces = numRows - 1;

        for (int row = 1; row <= numRows; row++) {
            for (int space = 1; space <= spaces; space++) {
                System.out.print(" ");
            }
            spaces--;

            for (int star = 1; star <= 2 * row - 1; star++) {
                System.out.print("*");
            }
            System.out.println();
        }
    }
}
```

### Inverted Right Half Pyramid

```
import java.util.*;

public class InvertedRightHalfPyramid {
    public static void main(String[] args) {
        Scanner scanner = new Scanner(System.in);

        System.out.print("Enter the number of rows: ");
        int numRows = scanner.nextInt();
            System.out.println();
        for (int row = numRows; row >= 1; row--) {
            for (int star = 1; star <= row; star++) {
                System.out.print("*");
            }
            System.out.println();
        }
    }
}
```

Section 12

# Pattern Printing Contd.

# Printing an Hourglass Pattern of Stars

## Introduction

Creating patterns with stars is a common exercise in programming. In this article, we will focus on printing an hourglass pattern of stars using java. We will discuss the understanding of the pattern, the approach to constructing it, and provide a step-by-step solution with sample code.

## Understanding the Hourglass Pattern of Stars

An hourglass pattern is a symmetric pattern that resembles the shape of an hourglass. It consists of rows of stars, gradually increasing and then decreasing in number, with a middle row containing the maximum number of stars.

## Approach

To print an hourglass pattern of stars, we can follow the following approach:

1. Determine the number of rows in the pattern based on the desired size.
2. Use nested loops to iterate through the rows and columns.
3. Print the desired number of spaces followed by stars in each row, aligning them to the centre.

## Step-by-Step Solution

1. Input the desired number of rows for the hourglass pattern.
2. Use a loop to iterate through each row from 1 to the desired number of rows:

    a. Use another loop to print the spaces before the stars.

    b. Print the desired number of spaces.

    c. Use another loop to print the stars.

    d. Print a star for each column up to the current row number, followed by another star for the next column.

3. After printing the upper half of the hourglass, repeat the same process for the lower half by reversing the loop range.
4. After printing all the rows, the hourglass pattern will be displayed.

## ➢ Printing an Hourglass Pattern of Stars ➣

```
import java.util.*;
public class HourglassPattern {
    public static void main(String[] args) {
        Scanner scanner = new Scanner(System.in);
        System.out.print("Enter the number of rows: ");
        int numRows = scanner.nextInt();
        System.out.println();
        int spaces = 0;
        // Print upper half
        for (int row = 1; row <= numRows; row++) {
            for (int space = 1; space <= spaces; space++) {
                System.out.print(" ");
            }
            spaces++;

            for (int star = 1; star <= 2 * (numRows - row) + 1; star++) {
                System.out.print("*");
            }
            System.out.println();
        }
        // Print lower half
        spaces = numRows - 1;
        for (int row = numRows - 1; row >= 1; row--) {
            for (int space = 1; space < spaces; space++) {
                System.out.print(" ");
            }
            spaces--;
            for (int star = 1; star <= 2 * (numRows - row) + 1; star++) {
                System.out.print("*");
            }
            System.out.println();
        }
    }
}
```

## Example Output

For numRows = 5, the output will be:

```
*****
 ***
  *
 ***
*****
```

# Printing a Hollow Square Pattern of Stars

## Introduction

Creating patterns with stars is a common exercise in programming. In this article, we will focus on printing a hollow square pattern of stars using java. We will discuss the understanding of the pattern, the approach to constructing it, and provide a step-by-step solution with sample code.

## Understanding the Hollow Square Pattern of Stars

A hollow square pattern is a pattern that consists of rows and columns of stars, forming a square shape with empty spaces in the middle. The outer border is made up of stars, while the inner area remains empty.

## Approach

To print a hollow square pattern of stars, we can follow the following approach:

1. Determine the size of the square pattern based on the desired number of rows or columns.
2. Use nested loops to iterate through the rows and columns.
3. Print the desired number of stars in each row, taking into account the special cases for the outer and inner rows.

## Step-by-Step Solution

1. Input the desired size of the square pattern.
2. Use a loop to iterate through each row from 1 to the desired size:
    - Use another loop to iterate through each column from 1 to the desired size
        1. For the first and last rows (outer rows), print a star for each column.
        2. For the remaining rows (inner rows), print a star for the first and last column, and empty spaces for the other columns.
3. After printing all the rows, the hollow square pattern will be displayed.

## ➢ Printing a Hollow Square Pattern of Stars ➣

## Code

Here's an example implementation for printing a hollow square pattern of stars:

```
import java.util.*;

    public class HollowSquarePattern {
        public static void main(String[] args) {
            Scanner scanner = new Scanner(System.in);

            System.out.print("Enter the size of the square pattern: ");
            int size = scanner.nextInt();
            System.out.println();
            for (int row = 1; row <= size; row++) {
                for (int col = 1; col <= size; col++) {
                    if (row == 1 || row == size || col == 1 || col == size) {
                        System.out.print("*");
                    } else {
                        System.out.print(" ");
                    }
                }
                System.out.println();
            }
        }
    }
```

## Example Output

For size = 5, the output will be:

```
*****
*   *
*   *
*   *
*****
```

# Ch 55

# Printing a Hollow Full Pyramid Pattern of Stars

## Introduction

Creating patterns with stars is a common exercise in programming. In this article, we will focus on printing a hollow full pyramid pattern of stars. We will discuss the understanding of the pattern, the approach to constructing it, and provide a step-by-step solution with sample code.

## Understanding the Hollow Full Pyramid Pattern of Stars

A hollow full pyramid pattern is a pattern that consists of rows and columns of stars, forming a pyramid shape with empty spaces in the middle. The outer border and inner structure of the pyramid are made up of stars, while the inner area remains empty.

## Approach

To print a hollow full pyramid pattern of stars, we can follow the following approach:

1. Determine the size of the pyramid pattern based on the desired number of rows.
2. Use nested loops to iterate through the rows and columns.
3. Print the desired number of spaces followed by stars in each row, taking into account the special cases for the outer and inner rows.

## Step-by-Step Solution

1. Input the desired number of rows for the pyramid pattern.
2. Use a loop to iterate through each row from 1 to the desired number of rows:
    a. Use another loop to print the desired number of spaces before the stars.
    b. Print a star for the first column and the last column.
    c. For the remaining columns, print a space if it is an outer column or a star if it is an inner column.
3. After printing all the rows, the hollow full pyramid pattern will be displayed.

## Code

Here's an example implementation for printing a hollow full pyramid pattern of stars:

```
import java.util.*;

public class HollowFullPyramid {
    public static void main(String[] args) {
        Scanner scanner = new Scanner(System.in);

        System.out.print("Enter the number of rows: ");
        int numRows = scanner.nextInt();
        System.out.println();

        for (int row = 1; row <= numRows; row++) {
            for (int space = 1; space <= numRows - row; space++) {
                System.out.print(" ");
            }

            for (int col = 1; col <= 2 * row - 1; col++) {
                if (col == 1 || col == 2 * row - 1 || row == numRows) {
                    System.out.print("*");
                } else {
                    System.out.print(" ");
                }
            }

            System.out.println();
        }
    }
}
```

## Example Output

For numRows = 5, the output will be:

```
    *
   * *
  *   *
 *     *
*********
```

# Printing a Hollow Diamond Pattern of Stars

## Introduction

Creating patterns with stars is a common exercise in programming. In this article, we will focus on printing a hollow diamond pattern of stars using java. We will discuss the understanding of the pattern, the approach to constructing it, and provide a step-by-step solution with sample code.

## Understanding the Hollow Diamond Pattern of Stars

A hollow diamond pattern is a pattern that consists of rows and columns of stars, forming a diamond shape with empty spaces in the middle and along the edges.

## Approach

To print a hollow diamond pattern of stars, we can follow the following approach:

1. Determine the size of the diamond pattern based on the desired number of rows or columns.
2. Use nested loops to iterate through the rows and columns.
3. Print the desired number of spaces followed by stars in each row, taking into account the special cases for the outer and inner rows.

## Step-by-Step Solution

1. Input the desired size of the diamond pattern.
2. Use a loop to iterate through each row from 1 to the desired size:
    a. Use another loop to print the desired number of spaces before the stars.
    b. Print a star for the first and last column.
    c. For the remaining columns, print a space if it is an outer column or a star if it is an inner column.
3. After printing the upper half of the diamond, repeat the same process for the lower half by reversing the loop range.
4. After printing all the rows, the hollow diamond pattern will be displayed.

## Code

Here's an example implementation for printing a hollow diamond pattern of stars:

```
import java.util.*;
public class HollowDiamondPattern {
    public static void main(String[] args) {
        Scanner scanner = new Scanner(System.in);
        System.out.print("Enter the size of the diamond pattern: ");
        int size = scanner.nextInt();
        System.out.println();
        for (int row = 1; row <= size; row++) {
            for (int space = 1; space <= size - row; space++) {
                System.out.print(" ");
            }
            for (int col = 1; col <= 2 * row - 1; col++) {
                if (col == 1 || col == 2 * row - 1) {
                    System.out.print("*");
                } else {
                    System.out.print(" ");
                }
            }
            System.out.println();
        }
        for (int row = size - 1; row >= 1; row--) {
            for (int space = 1; space <= size - row; space++) {
                System.out.print(" ");
            }
            for (int col = 1; col <= 2 * row - 1; col++) {
                if (col == 1 || col == 2 * row - 1) {
                    System.out.print("*");
                } else {
                    System.out.print(" ");
                }
            }
            System.out.println();
        }
    }
}
```

## Example Output

For size = 5, the output will be:

```
    *
   * *
  *   *
 *     *
*       *
 *     *
  *   *
   * *
    *
```

# Ch 57

# Floyd's Triangle Pattern

## Introduction

Floyd's Triangle is a specific number pattern that forms a triangular shape. Each row in the triangle contains a sequence of numbers, starting from 1 and incrementing by 1 for each subsequent row. In this chapter, we will explore Floyd's Triangle pattern, understand its construction, discuss the approach to solving it, and provide a step-by-step solution with sample code.

## Understanding Floyd's Triangle Pattern

Floyd's Triangle is a right-angled triangular pattern where each row contains consecutive numbers starting from 1. The number of elements in each row increases by 1 as we move down the triangle. It is named after Robert W. Floyd, an American computer scientist who introduced this pattern.

## Approach

To print Floyd's Triangle pattern, we can follow the following approach:

1. Input the desired number of rows for the triangle pattern.
2. Use nested loops to iterate through the rows and columns.
3. Initialize a variable with the value 1 to keep track of the numbers.
4. Print the current number and increment it after printing each element.

5. Ensure proper spacing and alignment of numbers to maintain the triangular shape.

### Step-by-Step Solution

- Input the desired number of rows for the Floyd's Triangle pattern.
- Initialize a variable num with the value 1.
- Use a loop to iterate through each row from 1 to the desired number of rows:
- Use another loop to iterate through the columns from 1 to the current row number.
- Print the value of num with appropriate spacing.
- Increment the value of num after printing each element.
- After printing all the rows, the Floyd's Triangle pattern will be displayed.

### Code

Here's an example implementation for printing Floyd's Triangle pattern:

```
import java.util.*;

public class FloydsTriangle {
    public static void main(String[] args) {
        Scanner scanner = new Scanner(System.in);

        System.out.print("Enter the number of rows for Floyd's Triangle pattern: ");
        int numRows = scanner.nextInt();

        int num = 1;
        for (int row = 1; row <= numRows; row++) {
            for (int col = 1; col <= row; col++) {
                System.out.print(num + " ");
                num++;
            }
            System.out.println();
        }
    }
}
```

Example Output

For numRows = 5, the output will be:

```
1
2 3
4 5 6
7 8 9 10
11 12 13 14 15
```

# Revision

## An Hourglass Pattern

```
import java.util.*;
public class HourglassPattern {
    public static void main(String[] args) {
        Scanner scanner = new Scanner(System.in);
        System.out.print("Enter the number of rows: ");
        int numRows = scanner.nextInt();
        System.out.println();
        int spaces = 0;
        // Print upper half
        for (int row = 1; row <= numRows; row++) {
            for (int space = 1; space <= spaces; space++) {
                System.out.print(" ");
            }
            spaces++;

            for (int star = 1; star <= 2 * (numRows - row) + 1; star++) {
                System.out.print("*");
            }
            System.out.println();
        }
        // Print lower half
        spaces = numRows - 1;
        for (int row = numRows - 1; row >= 1; row--) {
            for (int space = 1; space < spaces; space++) {
                System.out.print(" ");
            }
            spaces--;
            for (int star = 1; star <= 2 * (numRows - row) + 1; star++) {
                System.out.print("*");
            }
            System.out.println();
        }
    }
}
```

## Hollow Square Pattern

```
import java.util.*;

    public class HollowSquarePattern {
        public static void main(String[] args) {
            Scanner scanner = new Scanner(System.in);

            System.out.print("Enter the size of the square pattern: ");
            int size = scanner.nextInt();
            System.out.println();
            for (int row = 1; row <= size; row++) {
                for (int col = 1; col <= size; col++) {
                    if (row == 1 || row == size || col == 1 || col == size) {
                        System.out.print("*");
                    } else {
                        System.out.print(" ");
                    }
                }
                System.out.println();
            }
        }
    }
```

## Hollow Full Pyramid Pattern

```
import java.util.*;

public class HollowFullPyramid {
    public static void main(String[] args) {
        Scanner scanner = new Scanner(System.in);

        System.out.print("Enter the number of rows: ");
        int numRows = scanner.nextInt();
        System.out.println();

        for (int row = 1; row <= numRows; row++) {
            for (int space = 1; space <= numRows - row; space++) {
                System.out.print(" ");
            }

            for (int col = 1; col <= 2 * row - 1; col++) {
                if (col == 1 || col == 2 * row - 1 || row == numRows) {
                    System.out.print("*");
                } else {
                    System.out.print(" ");
                }
            }

            System.out.println();
        }
    }
}
```

## Hollow Diamond Pattern

```
import java.util.*;
public class HollowDiamondPattern {
    public static void main(String[] args) {
        Scanner scanner = new Scanner(System.in);
        System.out.print("Enter the size of the diamond pattern: ");
        int size = scanner.nextInt();
        System.out.println();
        for (int row = 1; row <= size; row++) {
            for (int space = 1; space <= size - row; space++) {
                System.out.print(" ");
            }
            for (int col = 1; col <= 2 * row - 1; col++) {
                if (col == 1 || col == 2 * row - 1) {
                    System.out.print("*");
                } else {
                    System.out.print(" ");
                }
            }
            System.out.println();
        }
        for (int row = size - 1; row >= 1; row--) {
            for (int space = 1; space <= size - row; space++) {
                System.out.print(" ");
            }
            for (int col = 1; col <= 2 * row - 1; col++) {
                if (col == 1 || col == 2 * row - 1) {
                    System.out.print("*");
                } else {
                    System.out.print(" ");
                }
            }
            System.out.println();
        }
    }
}
```

## Floyd's Triangle Pattern

```
import java.util.*;

public class FloydsTriangle {
    public static void main(String[] args) {
        Scanner scanner = new Scanner(System.in);

        System.out.print("Enter the number of rows for Floyd's Triangle pattern: ");
        int numRows = scanner.nextInt();

        int num = 1;
        for (int row = 1; row <= numRows; row++) {
            for (int col = 1; col <= row; col++) {
                System.out.print(num + " ");
                num++;
            }
            System.out.println();
        }
    }
}
```

Section 13

# Understanding Java Architecture

Ch 58

# Java Architecture

## Introduction

Java is one of the most popular programming languages in the world, known for its versatility, robustness, and platform independence. Behind the scenes, Java relies on a well-designed architecture that encompasses various components and layers. In this chapter, we will delve into the intricacies of Java architecture, exploring its foundations, core components, and how they work together to power the Java platform.

## Understanding Java Architecture

Java architecture refers to the overall structure and organization of the Java platform, including the runtime environment, virtual machine, libraries, and development tools. It provides the necessary framework for executing Java programs and enables cross-platform compatibility.

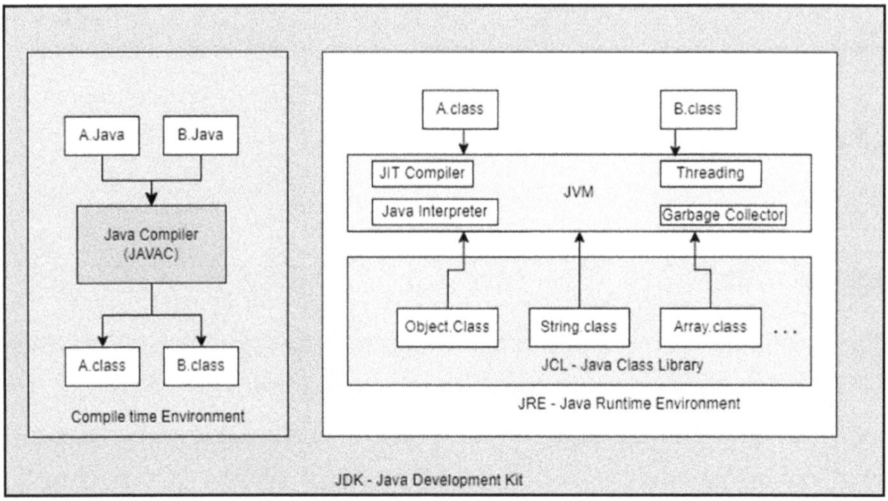


## Components of Java Architecture

### 1. Java Development Kit (JDK)

The JDK is a software development kit that includes tools, libraries, and documentation for developing Java applications. It provides compilers, debuggers, and other utilities essential for writing, compiling, and running Java code.

### 2. Java Virtual Machine (JVM)

The JVM is a key component of the Java architecture. It is responsible for executing Java bytecode, which is the compiled form of Java source code. The JVM abstracts the underlying hardware and operating system, providing a platform-independent runtime environment.

### 3. Java Runtime Environment (JRE)

The JRE includes the JVM along with the necessary libraries and resources required to run Java applications. It provides the runtime environment for executing Java programs, without the need for the development tools provided by the JDK.

### 4. Java Class Libraries

Java comes with an extensive set of class libraries, known as the Java Class Library (JCL). These libraries contain pre-defined classes and methods that developers can leverage to build applications. The JCL covers a wide range of functionalities, including input/output operations, networking, data structures, and graphical user interfaces.

### 5. Java Application Programming Interfaces (APIs)

Java APIs provide a set of classes, interfaces, and protocols that define how programmers can interact with the Java platform. The APIs offer a standardized way to access various functionalities, such as database connectivity, web services, XML processing, and more. They allow developers to leverage existing code and simplify application development.

## How Java Architecture Works

### 1. Compilation

Java source code is written in plain text files with a.java extension. The code is then compiled using the Java compiler (javac), which converts it into bytecode (.class files). The bytecode is platform-independent and can be executed on any system that has a compatible JVM.

### 2. Loading and Verification

The JVM loads the bytecode into memory and performs verification to ensure its integrity and security. It checks for errors, such as type mismatches and access violations, to prevent potential runtime issues.

### 3. Execution

The JVM executes the bytecode line by line using its internal interpreter or just-in-time (JIT) compiler. The interpreter translates bytecode into machine instructions on-the-fly, while the JIT compiler dynamically compiles frequently executed bytecode into native machine code for improved performance.

### 4. Memory Management

Java employs automatic memory management through the JVM's garbage collector. The garbage collector tracks objects in memory and frees up resources for objects that are no longer in use, relieving developers from manual memory management tasks.

### 5. Library Utilization

Developers leverage the Java Class Libraries and APIs to access pre-built functionality and implement desired features in their applications. These libraries provide a vast array of tools, utilities, and frameworks to simplify development tasks and enhance productivity.

# Java Development Kit (JDK)

## Introduction

The Java Development Kit (JDK) is a software development environment that provides tools, libraries, and components for developing Java applications. In this chapter, we will explore the JDK, understand its components, and discuss its importance in Java development. We will also cover the installation process and provide an overview of some key features.

## Understanding the Java Development Kit (JDK)

The JDK is a bundle of software tools and resources necessary for developing Java applications. It includes a set of libraries, a Java Virtual Machine (JVM), and various development tools such as compilers, debuggers, and documentation. The JDK is available for multiple platforms, including Windows, macOS, and Linux.

## Components of the JDK

### 1. Java Compiler

The JDK includes the Java compiler (javac), which translates Java source code into bytecode that can be executed by the JVM.

### 2. Java Virtual Machine (JVM)

The JVM is a key component of the JDK. It provides an environment for executing Java applications by interpreting bytecode or just-in-time (JIT) compiling it into machine code.

### 3. Java Runtime Environment (JRE)

The JDK includes the JRE, which is necessary for running Java applications. It contains the JVM and other runtime libraries required for executing Java programs.

### 4. Development Tools

The JDK provides various development tools, such as the Java Debugger (jdb) for debugging, the JavaDoc tool for generating documentation, and the Java Archive (JAR) tool for packaging Java applications.

### 5. Libraries

The JDK includes a vast collection of standard Java libraries (also known as the Java Class Library or Java API). These libraries provide pre-built functionality for common tasks, such as file handling, networking, and database access.

## Installing the JDK

To install the JDK, follow these steps:

1. Visit the official Oracle JDK website or the OpenJDK website.
2. Download the appropriate JDK distribution for your operating system.
3. Run the installer and follow the on-screen instructions to complete the installation.
4. Set the necessary environment variables, such as JAVA_HOME, to ensure proper functioning of the JDK.

## Key Features and Benefits of the JDK

### 1. Platform Independence

The JDK allows developers to write Java code once and run it on any platform that supports Java.

### 2. Robustness and Security

The JDK provides built-in features for handling exceptions, memory management, and security, ensuring reliable and secure application development.

### 3. Rich Standard Library

The JDK's extensive library collection simplifies development by offering ready-to-use components for common programming tasks.

### 4. Development Tools

The JDK's development tools streamline the coding process, providing features like debugging, profiling, and documentation generation.

# Java Runtime Environment

## Introduction

Java is a versatile and popular programming language used for developing a wide range of applications. To run Java programs, the Java Runtime Environment (JRE) is essential. In this article, we will explore the Java Runtime Environment, its components, functionalities, and its significance in Java application execution.

## Understanding the Java Runtime Environment (JRE)

The Java Runtime Environment (JRE) is a software package provided by Oracle Corporation that enables the execution of Java applications. It includes the necessary runtime libraries, Java Virtual Machine (JVM), and other components required to run Java programs. The JRE ensures platform independence by providing an environment where Java applications can run consistently across different operating systems and architectures.

## Components of the Java Runtime Environment

The JRE consists of several components, including:

### 1. Java Virtual Machine (JVM)

The JVM is the heart of the JRE. It is responsible for executing Java bytecode, which is the compiled form of Java programs. The JVM interprets the bytecode and provides a runtime environment for Java applications to run.

### 2. Java Class Library

The Java Class Library is a collection of pre-compiled classes and packages that provide a wide range of functionality to Java applications. It includes standard classes, data structures, utilities, and APIs for tasks such as file I/O, networking, database access, user interface development, and more.

### 3. Java Runtime Environment Configuration Files

The JRE contains configuration files that control various runtime settings, such as memory allocation, security policies, and class loading behaviour. These files can be customized to suit specific application requirements.

## Functionality of the Java Runtime Environment

The JRE provides the following key functionalities:

### 1. Java Application Execution

The JRE allows Java applications to be executed on any platform that supports the JRE. This platform independence is one of the key strengths of Java.

### 2. Memory Management

The JRE manages memory allocation and deallocation, ensuring efficient utilization of system resources. It includes automatic memory management through garbage collection, which frees up memory occupied by objects no longer in use.

### 3. Platform Integration

The JRE integrates with the underlying operating system to provide a consistent runtime environment for Java applications. It abstracts the differences between operating systems, allowing Java programs to run seamlessly across platforms.

### 4. Security

The JRE includes security features that protect against unauthorized access, data breaches, and malicious code execution. It provides mechanisms for sandboxing, access control, and encryption to ensure the safety and integrity of Java applications.

## Significance of the Java Runtime Environment

The JRE plays a crucial role in Java application execution and enables the widespread adoption of Java as a programming language. It allows developers to write code once and run it anywhere, simplifying the development and deployment process. The JRE's robustness, platform independence, memory management, and security features make it a reliable and trusted environment for running Java applications.

# Java Virtual Machine (JVM)

## Introduction

The Java Virtual Machine (JVM) is a crucial component of the Java platform that plays a vital role in executing Java applications. In this article, we will explore the JVM, understand its purpose, architecture, and working principles. We will delve into its key features and benefits, as well as discuss its role in enabling platform independence and optimizing performance.

## Understanding the Java Virtual Machine (JVM)

The JVM is a virtual machine that provides an execution environment for Java applications. It acts as an intermediary between the Java code and the underlying hardware and operating system. The JVM enables Java programs to run on any platform that supports it, without the need for recompilation.

## JVM Components

The JVM consists of several key components:

### 1. Class Loader

The class loader is responsible for loading Java class files into memory. It searches for the required classes and dynamically loads them as needed.

### 2. Bytecode Verifier

The bytecode verifier ensures the integrity and security of Java programs. It verifies that the bytecode conforms to the Java language specifications and prevents any potentially harmful operations.

### 3. Just-in-Time (JIT) Compiler

The JIT compiler is a key component of the JVM that improves performance. It dynamically analyses the bytecode and selectively compiles frequently executed code into native machine code for efficient execution.

### 4. Garbage Collector

The JVM includes a garbage collector that manages memory allocation and deallocation. It automatically reclaims memory that is no longer in use, freeing developers from manual memory management.

### 5. Execution Engine

The execution engine executes the compiled bytecode. It includes an interpreter that executes the bytecode line by line and a JIT compiler that optimizes performance by compiling frequently executed code into native machine code.

## JVM Working Principles:

### 1. Loading

The JVM loads Java class files into memory as they are needed during program execution. It follows a three-step process: loading, linking, and initialization.

2. **Verifying**

The JVM verifies the bytecode to ensure type safety and security. It checks for any violations of the Java language rules and prevents potentially harmful operations.

3. **Executing**

The JVM executes the bytecode using the execution engine. It can either interpret the bytecode line by line or compile it into native machine code for optimized performance.

4. **Garbage Collection**

The JVM manages memory allocation and deallocation through automatic garbage collection. It identifies and collects objects that are no longer reachable, freeing up memory for future use.

5. **Performance Optimization**

The JVM optimizes performance through techniques such as Just-in-Time (JIT) compilation. It identifies hotspots in the code and compiles them into native machine code for faster execution.

**Benefits of the JVM:**

1. **Platform Independence**

The JVM enables Java programs to run on any platform that supports it, without the need for recompilation. This platform independence is a significant advantage of Java.

2. **Memory Management**

The JVM automates memory management, relieving developers from the burden of manual memory allocation and deallocation. The garbage collector efficiently manages memory resources.

### 3. Performance Optimization

The JVM's Just-in-Time (JIT) compilation and runtime optimization techniques improve the performance of Java applications by dynamically compiling frequently executed code.

### 4. Security

The JVM's bytecode verifier ensures the security and integrity of Java programs by validating bytecode against the Java language specifications, preventing malicious or unsafe operations.

# Java Class Libraries

## Introduction

Java is a powerful and versatile programming language known for its vast collection of class libraries. These libraries, collectively known as the Java Class Libraries, provide developers with a wide range of pre-built classes and functions that simplify application development. In this article, we will explore the Java Class Libraries, their significance, and how they enhance the Java development experience.

## Understanding Java Class Libraries

Java Class Libraries are a comprehensive set of reusable classes, interfaces, and APIs that come bundled with the Java Development Kit (JDK). These libraries provide a wealth of functionality that covers various domains, including networking, file I/O, database connectivity, graphical user interfaces (GUI), data structures, cryptography, and more. They serve as a foundation for building Java applications, offering ready-to-use components and tools to developers.

## Significance of Java Class Libraries

The Java Class Libraries offer several significant benefits to Java developers:

1. **Reusability**

The libraries contain a vast collection of pre-built classes and functions that developers can utilize in their applications. This promotes code reusability, allowing developers to leverage existing code rather than reinventing the wheel. By using the Java Class Libraries, developers can save time and effort while maintaining consistent and reliable code.

2. **Faster Development**

The extensive range of classes and APIs in the libraries accelerates the development process. Developers can utilize high-level abstractions and built-in functionalities to simplify complex tasks, reducing development time and increasing productivity. The libraries handle low-level operations, allowing developers to focus on application logic rather than implementation details.

3. **Standardization**

The Java Class Libraries follow a set of industry-standard interfaces and conventions. This ensures that Java applications built using these libraries are portable and compatible across different platforms and Java Virtual Machines (JVMs). The standardized APIs provide a consistent development experience, making it easier for developers to collaborate and maintain codebases.

4. **Reliability and Security**

The Java Class Libraries undergo rigorous testing and maintenance by the Java community and Oracle Corporation. This ensures their reliability, stability, and security. By leveraging the libraries, developers can benefit from proven and trusted solutions, reducing the likelihood of bugs and vulnerabilities in their applications.

## Exploring Java Class Libraries

The Java Class Libraries encompass several core packages, such as java.lang, java.util, java.io, java.net, java.sql, java.awt, javax.swing, and more. Each package focuses on specific functionality and provides a set of related classes and interfaces. For example, the java. util package includes classes for working with collections, dates, and times, while the java.net package offers classes for networking operations.

Developers can explore the Java Class Libraries documentation to gain insight into available classes, interfaces, and their respective functionalities. They can leverage the libraries by importing the required packages into their Java code and utilizing the provided classes and methods.

# Java Application Programming Interfaces

## Introduction

Java is a versatile programming language known for its rich set of Application Programming Interfaces (APIs). APIs provide a standardized way for developers to interact with various software components, libraries, and services. In this article, we will explore Java APIs, their significance, and how they serve as building blocks for Java application development.

## Understanding Java APIs:

An Application Programming Interface (API) is a set of rules and protocols that define how software components should interact with each other. Java APIs, specifically, are collections of classes, interfaces, and methods that provide ready-to-use functionality for developers. These APIs are organized into packages, each focusing on a specific domain or functionality.

## Significance of Java APIs

Java APIs offer several significant benefits to Java developers:

### 1. Code Reusability

APIs provide a set of pre-built classes and methods that developers can use in their applications. By utilizing APIs, developers can leverage existing code, saving time and effort in development. This promotes code reusability, ensuring consistency and reducing the chances of introducing bugs.

## 2. Standardization

Java APIs follow a set of well-defined standards and conventions, ensuring compatibility across different Java implementations and platforms. Developers can rely on these standards to build portable and interoperable applications. The standardized APIs also make it easier for developers to collaborate and share code.

## 3. Increased Productivity

APIs simplify complex tasks by encapsulating functionality into easy-to-use methods and classes. Developers can focus on application logic rather than low-level implementation details. By using APIs, developers can accelerate development, improve productivity, and deliver high-quality code more efficiently.

## 4. Ecosystem Support

Java APIs are supported by a vast ecosystem of libraries, frameworks, and tools. These resources provide additional functionality and extend the capabilities of Java applications. Developers can leverage popular libraries and frameworks built on top of Java APIs to enhance their applications with advanced features and functionalities.

## Exploring Java APIs

Java APIs cover a wide range of domains, including networking, file handling, database connectivity, graphical user interfaces, multithreading, and more. Some commonly used Java APIs include java.util, java.io, java.net, java.sql, java.awt, javax.swing, and many others. Each API package provides a set of classes and methods that serve specific purposes.

Developers can access and utilize Java APIs by importing the required packages into their Java code. They can then create instances of classes, invoke methods, and utilize the provided functionality to build robust and feature-rich applications.

# Memory Management

## Introduction

Efficient memory management is a crucial aspect of any programming language, and Java has a robust memory management system in place. In this article, we will explore memory management in Java, including its importance, the Java memory model, garbage collection, and best practices for optimizing memory usage.

## Understanding Memory Management in Java

Memory management in Java involves allocating and deallocating memory for objects during runtime. Unlike languages like C or C++, Java handles memory management automatically, alleviating developers from manually managing memory allocation and deallocation. This automatic memory management is achieved through the Java Virtual Machine (JVM) and the garbage collector.

## Java Memory Model

The Java memory model is responsible for managing the different types of memory areas in a Java program:

### 1. Heap Memory

The heap memory is where objects are dynamically allocated during runtime. It is the primary area of focus for memory management in Java. Objects created using the "new" keyword are stored in the heap.

## 2. Stack Memory

The stack memory is used for storing local variables and method call information. Each thread in a Java program has its own stack memory. The stack memory is managed by the JVM and is automatically freed when a method or thread finishes execution.

## 3. Method Area

The method area stores class-level information, including bytecode, static variables, and constant pool. It is shared among all threads and contains information about loaded classes and their methods.

## Garbage Collection

Garbage collection is a core component of memory management in Java. The garbage collector identifies and reclaims memory occupied by objects that are no longer in use, freeing up resources and preventing memory leaks. The JVM's garbage collector automatically handles the process of deallocating memory.

The garbage collector uses a mark-and-sweep algorithm, where it marks objects that are still in use and sweeps away objects that are no longer referenced. It traverses the object graph starting from the root objects (such as static variables, method parameters, and thread stacks) and marks objects that are reachable. Any objects that are not marked as reachable are considered garbage and can be safely collected.

## Memory Management Best Practices

To optimize memory usage in Java, consider the following best practices:

1. **Use Objects Wisely**

Create objects only when necessary and avoid excessive object creation. Be mindful of object lifetimes and ensure objects are released when they are no longer needed.

2. **Nullify Unused References**

Set object references to null when they are no longer needed. This allows the garbage collector to reclaim memory occupied by unreferenced objects.

3. **Avoid Memory Leaks**

Ensure that objects are properly released and references are cleared. Avoid circular references that can prevent objects from being garbage collected.

4. **Use Proper Collection Types**

Choose the appropriate collection types (such as ArrayList, HashMap, etc.) based on your requirements. Consider the performance characteristics and memory usage of different collection types.

5. **Monitor and Tune Garbage Collection**

Understand the behaviour of the garbage collector in your JVM implementation. Monitor memory usage and analyse garbage collection logs to identify any potential issues. Tune the garbage collector parameters if necessary.

## Revision

**Components of Java Architecture**

1. Java Development Kit (JDK)
2. Java Virtual Machine (JVM)
3. Java Runtime Environment (JRE)
4. Java Class Libraries
5. Java Application Programming Interfaces (APIs)

**How Java Architecture Works**

1. Compilation
2. Loading and Verification
3. Execution
4. Memory Management
5. Library Utilization

**Components of the JDK**

1. Java Compiler
2. Java Virtual Machine (JVM)
3. Java Runtime Environment (JRE)
4. Development Tools
5. Libraries

**Installing the JDK**

1. Visit the official Oracle JDK website or the OpenJDK website.
2. Download the appropriate JDK distribution for your operating system.

3. Run the installer and follow the on-screen instructions to complete the installation.
4. Set the necessary environment variables, such as JAVA_HOME, to ensure proper functioning of the JDK.

## Java Runtime Environment

The Java Runtime Environment (JRE) is a software package provided by Oracle Corporation that enables the execution of Java applications. It includes the necessary runtime libraries, Java Virtual Machine (JVM), and other components required to run Java programs. The JRE ensures platform independence by providing an environment where Java applications can run consistently across different operating systems and architectures.

## Java Virtual Machine

The JVM is a virtual machine that provides an execution environment for Java applications. It acts as an intermediary between the Java code and the underlying hardware and operating system. The JVM enables Java programs to run on any platform that supports it, without the need for recompilation.

## Components of JVM

1. Class Loader
2. Bytecode Verifier
3. Just-in-Time (JIT) Compiler
4. Garbage Collector
5. Execution Engine

## JVM Working Principles

1. Loading
2. Verifying
3. Executing
4. Garbage Collection
5. Performance Optimization

## Java Class Libraries

Java Class Libraries are a comprehensive set of reusable classes, interfaces, and APIs that come bundled with the Java Development Kit (JDK). These libraries provide a wealth of functionality that covers various domains, including networking, file I/O, database connectivity, graphical user interfaces (GUI), data structures, cryptography, and more. They serve as a foundation for building Java applications, offering ready-to-use components and tools to developers.

## Benefits of JCL

1. Reusability
2. Faster Development
3. Standardization
4. Reliability and Security

## Java Application Programming Interface APIs

An Application Programming Interface (API) is a set of rules and protocols that define how software components should interact with each other. Java APIs, specifically, are collections of classes, interfaces, and methods that provide ready-to-use functionality for developers. These APIs are organized into packages, each focusing on a specific domain or functionality.

## Memory Management

Memory management in Java involves allocating and deallocating memory for objects during runtime. Unlike languages like C or C++, Java handles memory management automatically, alleviating developers from manually managing memory allocation and deallocation. This automatic memory management is achieved through the Java Virtual Machine (JVM) and the garbage collector.

## Java Memory Model

1. Heap Memory
2. Stack Memory
3. Method Area

## Garbage Collection

Garbage collection is a core component of memory management in Java. The garbage collector identifies and reclaims memory occupied by objects that are no longer in use, freeing up resources and preventing memory leaks. The JVM's garbage collector automatically handles the process of deallocating memory.

Section 14

# Miscellaneous

# Ch 65

# Object Oriented Programming

## Introduction

Object-Oriented Programming (OOP) is a popular programming paradigm that revolutionized software development. It offers a powerful approach to designing and organizing code, making it more modular, reusable, and maintainable. In this article, we will explore the concepts, principles, and benefits of Object-Oriented Programming, along with practical examples. Object-Oriented Programming was introduced by Alan Kay somewhere in1960s. As per Alan Kay *"OOP to me means only messaging, local retention and protection and hiding of state-process, and extreme late-binding of all things."*

## Understanding Object-Oriented Programming

At its core, Object-Oriented Programming revolves around the concept of objects, which are instances of classes. Objects encapsulate data (attributes) and behaviour (methods) related to a specific entity. OOP promotes the organization of code into reusable building blocks, making it easier to model real-world entities and solve complex problems.

## Key Concepts in Object-Oriented Programming

### Classes

Classes are blueprints or templates that define the structure and behaviour of objects. They encapsulate attributes (data) and methods (functions) that represent the characteristics and actions of the objects.

### Objects

Objects are instances of classes. They are created based on the defined class blueprint and contain specific data values for the attributes defined in the class. Objects can perform operations by invoking the methods defined in their class.

### Abstraction

Abstraction means an idea in theory that can be implemented later or generalization of aspects of reality. Specifications can be provided later in reality. Abstraction can be referred to as modeling and is closely related to the concepts of theory and design. Modeling the relevant attributes and interactions of entities as classes to define an abstract representation of a system. Abstraction focuses on representing the essential characteristics of an object. Abstraction simplifies complex systems, promotes code modularity, and enhances code maintainability. Abstraction is the underlying principle behind the core pillars of OOP i.e. Encapsulation, Inheritance and Polymorphism

### Encapsulation

Encapsulation is the process of bundling data (attributes) and methods (functions) into a single unit called a class, hiding the internal implementation details. It protects the data from unauthorized access and ensures that the class's methods are the only way to interact with the data. Encapsulation ensures data integrity, enhances code maintainability, and enables information hiding, preventing direct manipulation of internal implementation details.

## Inheritance

Inheritance enables the creation of new classes (subclasses) based on existing classes (superclasses). Subclasses inherit attributes and methods from their superclasses, allowing code reuse and promoting the "is-a" relationship between classes. Inheritance provides a way to model and represent hierarchical relationships, enhances code extensibility, and allows for specialization and customization.

## Polymorphism

Polymorphism means "many forms" and refers to the ability of objects to take on different forms based on their context. Polymorphism allows objects of different classes to be treated as instances of a common superclass. It enables methods to be implemented differently in different subclasses while adhering to a common interface. Polymorphism promotes code flexibility and extensibility and enables the implementation of methods specific to each object type. It enables the use of a common interface to interact with different objects, regardless of their specific implementations. Polymorphism is achieved through method overriding and method overloading, enabling different implementations of methods with the same name.

## Benefits of Object-Oriented Programming

## Object-Oriented Programming offers several benefits for software development:

### Modularity and Reusability

OOP allows code to be organized into modular units (classes), making it easier to understand, test, and maintain. Classes can be reused in different parts of the program, reducing redundancy and promoting code efficiency.

### Code Organization

OOP provides a clear and intuitive structure for designing and organizing code. The division of functionality into classes and objects enables better code management and promotes teamwork.

### Scalability and Extensibility

OOP facilitates the addition of new features and modifications to existing code without impacting other parts of the program. This promotes code flexibility and adaptability, making it easier to handle complex software projects.

### Code Readability

OOP emphasizes the use of meaningful class and method names, making code more self-explanatory and easier to understand. It enhances code readability, reducing the time and effort required for maintenance and debugging.

### Practical Examples in Java

Let's illustrate some practical examples of OOP concepts using Java:

## Class and Object

```
public class Car {
  String brand;
  int year;

  void startEngine() {
      // Code to start the car's engine
  }

  void accelerate() {
      // Code to accelerate the car
  }
}

// Creating objects of the Car class
Car car1 = new Car();
Car car2 = new Car();
```

## Inheritance

```
public class Animal {
  void eat() {
      // Code for eating
  }
}

public class Dog extends Animal {
  void bark() {
      // Code for barking
  }
}

// Creating objects of the Dog class
Dog dog = new Dog();
dog.eat();  // Inherited method from Animal class
dog.bark();
```

## Polymorphism

```
public class Shape {
  void draw() {
      // Code to draw the shape
  }
}

public class Circle extends Shape {
  void draw() {
      // Code to draw a circle
  }
}

public class Rectangle extends Shape {
  void draw() {
      // Code to draw a rectangle
  }
}

// Creating objects of different shapes
Shape shape1 = new Circle();
Shape shape2 = new Rectangle();

shape1.draw();  // Calls the draw() method specific to a circle
shape2.draw();  // Calls the draw() method specific to a rectangle
```

Ch 66

# C++ Architecture

## Introduction

C++ is a widely used programming language known for its efficiency, flexibility, and extensive support for system-level programming. Behind the scenes, C++ relies on a well-designed architecture that encompasses various components and features. In this article, we will dive into the architecture of C++, exploring its foundations, key components, and how they work together to create powerful and performant applications.

## Understanding C++ Architecture

C++ architecture refers to the overall structure and organization of the C++ programming language, including its syntax, memory management, compilation process, and runtime environment. It provides the necessary framework for writing, compiling, and executing C++ programs.

## Components of C++ Architecture

### 1. Syntax

C++ is based on the syntax of the C programming language. It extends the C language with additional features such as classes, objects, and inheritance, providing support for object-oriented programming. The syntax of C++ is designed to be expressive and efficient, allowing developers to write code that is both readable and performant.

## 2. Compilation Process

The compilation process in C++ involves several stages. First, the source code is pre-processed, where directives like #include and macro definitions are processed. Then, the pre-processed code is compiled into object files by the C++ compiler. Finally, the object files are linked together to produce an executable file.

## 3. Memory Management

C++ gives developers control over memory management. It supports both automatic and manual memory allocation and deallocation. Automatic memory management is achieved through stack allocation, where variables are allocated and deallocated automatically when they go in and out of scope. Manual memory management is facilitated through dynamic memory allocation using operators such as new and delete.

## 4. Standard Template Library (STL)

The STL is a powerful component of C++ architecture that provides a collection of generic algorithms and data structures. It includes containers like vectors, lists, and maps, as well as algorithms for sorting, searching, and manipulating data. The STL enables developers to write efficient and reusable code by leveraging these pre-defined components.

## 5. Object-Oriented Programming (OOP) Features

C++ supports object-oriented programming paradigms, allowing developers to create classes, objects, and inheritance hierarchies. It provides features such as encapsulation, polymorphism, and inheritance, enabling modular and reusable code. The combination of OOP features with low-level control makes C++ a versatile language for various application domains.

### 6. Standard Library

The C++ Standard Library includes a rich set of functions and classes that extend the core language capabilities. It provides support for I/O operations, string manipulation, mathematical computations, concurrency, and more. The Standard Library allows developers to write efficient and portable code by relying on these standardized components.

### 7. Compiler

The C++ compiler is responsible for translating C++ source code into machine-readable instructions. It performs syntactic and semantic analysis, optimizes the code, and generates the corresponding executable or object files. Different compilers may have variations in terms of language support and optimization capabilities.

## How C++ Architecture Works

### 1. Development

Developers write C++ code using a text editor or an integrated development environment (IDE). They utilize the C++ syntax, object-oriented principles, and the Standard Library to implement desired functionalities.

### 2. Compilation

The C++ source code is fed into a C++ compiler, which performs lexical analysis, syntax parsing, and semantic analysis. It checks for syntax errors, resolves references, and type-checks the code. The output of this phase is an object file containing machine-readable instructions.

### 3. Linking

The object files generated during the compilation phase are linked together by a linker. The linker resolves references to external functions and libraries and generates the final executable file.

### 4. Execution

The generated executable can be run on the target platform, where the C++ runtime environment executes the program. The runtime environment manages memory, handles I/O operations, and ensures the proper execution of the C++ program.

# Exploring Java Frameworks

Java frameworks offer developers a set of pre-defined functionalities, libraries, and structures to simplify common tasks and promote best practices. Let's take a look at some of the most widely used Java frameworks:

## Spring Framework

The Spring Framework is one of the most popular Java frameworks, known for its versatility and comprehensive ecosystem. It provides support for building enterprise-level applications, web services, and microservices. Spring offers features like dependency injection, data access, security, and more. Here's an example:

*Link: Spring Framework - https://spring.io/*

```
import org.springframework.boot.SpringApplication;
import org.springframework.boot.autoconfigure.SpringBootApplication;

@SpringBootApplication
public class MyApp {
    public static void main(String[] args) {
        SpringApplication.run(MyApp.class, args);
    }
}
```

## Hibernate

Hibernate is an object-relational mapping (ORM) framework that simplifies database operations in Java applications. It allows you to interact with databases using plain Java objects, eliminating the need for complex SQL queries. Hibernate provides a powerful and intuitive way to manage database persistence. Here's an example:

*Link: Hibernate* - https://hibernate.org/

```
@Entity
@Table(name = "users")
public class User {
    @Id
    @GeneratedValue(strategy = GenerationType.IDENTITY)
    private Long id;

    private String name;
    private String email;
    // ...
}

public interface UserRepository extends JpaRepository {
    // Custom query methods...
}
```

## Apache Struts

Apache Struts is a popular web application framework used to build scalable and maintainable Java web applications. It follows the Model-View-Controller (MVC) architectural pattern and provides features for routing, validation, and data binding. Struts has been widely adopted in enterprise environments. Here's an example:

*Link: Apache Struts* - https://struts.apache.org/

```
public class HelloWorldAction extends ActionSupport {
    private String message;

    public String execute() throws Exception {
        message = "Hello, World!";
        return SUCCESS;
    }

    public String getMessage() {
        return message;
    }
}
```

## Apache Maven

Apache Maven is a powerful build automation and dependency management tool for Java projects. It simplifies the process of managing project dependencies, compiling code, running tests, and generating project documentation. Maven helps ensure consistency and reproducibility in your builds. Here's an example:

*Link: Apache Maven* - https://maven.apache.org/

```
<project xmlns="http://maven.apache.org/POM/4.0.0"
    xmlns:xsi="http://www.w3.org/2001/XMLSchema-instance"
    xsi:schemaLocation="http://maven.apache.org/POM/4.0.0 http://maven.apache.org/xsd/maven-
4.0.0.xsd">
    <modelVersion>4.0.0</modelVersion>
    <groupId>com.example</groupId>
    <artifactId>my-project</artifactId>
    <version>1.0.0</version>
    <!-- Dependencies, plugins, and other configurations... -->
</project>
```

# Bitwise Operators: AND, OR, XOR, and NOT

Bitwise operations are fundamental to low-level programming and are extensively used in system programming, graphics, cryptography, and algorithm optimization. Understanding how to manipulate individual bits of data can yield more efficient and powerful code. This chapter delves into the core bitwise operators: AND, OR, XOR, and NOT, which are integral to manipulating binary data.

## Understanding Bitwise Operations

At their core, bitwise operations directly manipulate bits within a binary representation of numbers. They operate on binary digits (bits) of the operands and perform operations bit by bit.

### 1. Bitwise AND (&)

The bitwise AND operator compares each bit of its operands. If both bits are 1, the resulting bit is set to 1. Otherwise, it is set to 0.

Truth Table:

| A | B | A & B |
|---|---|---|
| 0 | 0 | 0 |
| 0 | 1 | 0 |
| 1 | 0 | 0 |
| 1 | 1 | 1 |

**Example**

```
int a = 12; // 1100 in binary
int b = 10; // 1010 in binary
int result = a & b; // 1000 in binary, which is 8 in decimal

System.out.println("Result of a & b: " + result); // Output: 8
```

## 2. Bitwise OR (|)

The bitwise OR operator compares each bit of its operands. If at least one of the bits is 1, the resulting bit is set to 1.

**Truth Table:**

| A | B | A \| B |
|---|---|---|
| 0 | 0 | 0 |
| 0 | 1 | 1 |
| 1 | 0 | 1 |
| 1 | 1 | 1 |

**Example**

```
int a = 12; // 1100 in binary
int b = 10; // 1010 in binary
int result = a | b; // 1110 in binary, which is 14 in decimal

System.out.println("Result of a | b: " + result); // Output: 14
```

## 3. Bitwise XOR (^)

The bitwise XOR operator compares each bit of its operands. If the bits are different, the resulting bit is set to 1. If they are the same, the resulting bit is set to 0.

Truth Table:

| A | B | A ^ B |
|---|---|---|
| 0 | 0 | 0 |
| 0 | 1 | 1 |
| 1 | 0 | 1 |
| 1 | 1 | 0 |

Example

```
int a = 12; // 1100 in binary
int b = 10; // 1010 in binary
int result = a ^ b; // 0110 in binary, which is 6 in decimal

System.out.println("Result of a ^ b: " + result); // Output: 6
```

## 4. Bitwise NOT (~)

The bitwise NOT operator inverts each bit of its operand. It turns 0s into 1s and 1s into 0s. The bitwise NOT is applied using two's complement representation, which means the result is the negative of the value incremented by one.

**Example**

```
int a = 12; // 1100 in binary
int result = ~a; // 0011 in binary for 4-bit representation, which is -13 in decimal

System.out.println("Result of ~a: " + result); // Output: -13
```

## Applications of Bitwise Operations

### 1. Efficient Computation

Bitwise operations are much faster than arithmetic operations, making them ideal for performance-critical applications such as encryption algorithms and graphic manipulations.

### 2. Bit Masking

Bitwise operations are used to create, modify, and read specific bits within a byte or word. For example, setting a particular bit can be done using OR, clearing a bit using AND, and toggling a bit using XOR.

### 3. Cryptography

Bitwise operations are foundational in cryptographic algorithms, which require manipulating individual bits to encrypt and decrypt data.

# Commutative and Associative Properties of Bitwise Operators

## Overview

Two fundamental properties of Bitwise operators are commutativity and associativity.

Let's briefly review the primary bitwise operators:

1. AND (&): Compares each bit of its operands, returning 1 if both bits are 1 and 0 otherwise.
2. OR (|): Compares each bit of its operands, returning 1 if at least one bit is 1 and 0 otherwise.
3. XOR (^): Compares each bit of its operands, returning 1 if the bits are different and 0 if they are the same.
4. NOT (~): Inverts all the bits of its operand.

## Commutative Property

The commutative property states that the order of the operands does not affect the result of the operation. For bitwise operators, this property applies to AND, OR, and XOR.

## Commutativity of AND

The commutative property for the AND operator can be expressed as:

$$A \,\&\, B = B \,\&\, A$$

**Example**

Consider $A = 5$ (binary: 0101) and $B = 3$ (binary: 0011)

$A \,\&\, B = 0101 \,\&\, 0011 = 0001 = 1$

$B \,\&\, A = 0011 \,\&\, 0101 = 0001 = 1$

Thus, $A \,\&\, B = B \,\&\, A$

**Commutativity of OR**

The commutative property for the OR operator can be expressed as:

$$A \mid B = B \mid A$$

**Example**

Using the same values $A = 5$ and $B = 3$:

$A \mid B = 0101 \mid 0011 = 0111 = 7$

$B \mid A = 0011 \mid 0101 = 0111 = 7$

Thus, $A \mid B = B \mid A$.

**Commutativity of XOR**

The commutative property for the XOR operator can be expressed as:

$$A \wedge B = B \wedge A$$

## Example

Using the same values $A = 5$ and $B = 3$:

$A \wedge B = 0101 \wedge 0011 = 0110 = 6$

$B \wedge A = 0011 \wedge 0101 = 0110 = 6$

Thus, $A \wedge B = B \wedge A$.

## Code Example

```
public class BitwiseCommutative {
    public static void main(String[] args) {
        int A = 5;
        int B = 3;

        System.out.println("A & B = " + (A & B));
        System.out.println("B & A = " + (B & A));

        System.out.println("A | B = " + (A | B));
        System.out.println("B | A = " + (B | A));

        System.out.println("A ^ B = " + (A ^ B));
        System.out.println("B ^ A = " + (B ^ A));
    }
}
```

## Associative Property

The associative property states that the grouping of operands does not affect the result of the operation. For bitwise operators, this property applies to AND, OR, and XOR.

## Associativity of AND

The associative property for the AND operator can be expressed as:

$$(A \,\&\, B) \,\&\, C = A \,\&\, (B \,\&\, C)$$

## Example

Consider $A$ = 5 (binary: 0101), $B$= 3 (binary: 0011), and $C$ = 6 (binary: 0110).

$$(A \,\&\, B) \,\&\, C = (0101 \,\&\, 0011) \,\&\, 0110 = 0001 \,\&\, 0110 = 0000 = 0$$

$$A \,\&\, (B \,\&\, C) = 0101 \,\&\, (0011 \,\&\, 0110) = 0101 \,\&\, 0010 = 0000 = 0$$

Thus, $(A \,\&\, B) \,\&\, C = A \,\&\, (B \,\&\, C)$.

## Associativity of OR

The associative property for the OR operator can be expressed as:

$$(A \mid B) \mid C = A \mid (B \mid C)$$

## Example

Using the same values $A$ = 5, $B$ = 3, and $C$ = 6:

$$(A \mid B) \mid C = (0101 \mid 0011) \mid 0110 = 0111 \mid 0110 = 0111 = 7$$

$$A \mid (B \mid C) = 0101 \mid (0011 \mid 0110) = 0101 \mid 0111 = 0111 = 7$$

Thus, $(A \mid B) \mid C = A \mid (B \mid C)$.

## Associativity of XOR

The associative property for the XOR operator can be expressed as:

$$(A \wedge B) \wedge C = A \wedge (B \wedge C)$$

## Example

Using the same values $A = 5$, $B = 3$, and $C = 6$:

$(A \wedge B) \wedge C = (0101 \wedge 0011) \wedge 0110 = 0110 \wedge 0110 = 0000 = 0$

$A \wedge (B \wedge C) = 0101 \wedge (0011 \wedge 0110) = 0101 \wedge 0101 = 0000 = 0$

Thus, $(A \wedge B) \wedge C = A \wedge (B \wedge C)$.

## Code Example

```
public class BitwiseAssociative {
    public static void main(String[] args) {
        int A = 5;
        int B = 3;
        int C = 6;

        System.out.println("(A & B) & C = " + ((A & B) & C));
        System.out.println("A & (B & C) = " + (A & (B & C)));

        System.out.println("(A | B) | C = " + ((A | B) | C));
        System.out.println("A | (B | C) = " + (A | (B | C)));

        System.out.println("(A ^ B) ^ C = " + ((A ^ B) ^ C));
        System.out.println("A ^ (B ^ C) = " + (A ^ (B ^ C)));
    }
}
```

# Finding Odd and Even Numbers Using Bitwise AND (&)

In this chapter, we will explore how the bitwise AND operator can be employed to determining whether a number is odd or even.

## Understanding Bitwise AND

The bitwise AND operator (&) compares each bit of its operands and returns a new binary number. Each bit in the resulting number is 1 if both corresponding bits in the operands are 1; otherwise, it is 0.

For example, 5 & 3 evaluates to 1 because:

- Binary representation of 5 is 101.
- Binary representation of 3 is 011.
- Performing bitwise AND results in 001, which is 1 in decimal.

## Determining Odd and Even Numbers

In binary representation, even numbers always end with 0 and odd numbers end with 1. This property allows us to use the bitwise AND operator to check the least significant bit (LSB) of a number. Specifically, we can use the number 1 (binary 0001) to isolate the LSB of any integer:

1. If a number is even, its LSB is 0, and performing a bitwise AND with 1 will yield 0.
2. If a number is odd, its LSB is 1, and performing a bitwise AND with 1 will yield 1.

## Example

Even number: 4 (binary 0100): 4 & 1 results in 0 because 0100 & 0001 is 0000.

Odd number: 7 (binary 0111): 7 & 1 results in 1 because 0111 & 0001 is 0001.

## Approach

1. Input: Accept an integer from the user.
2. Bitwise Operation: Use the bitwise AND operator with 1 to check the LSB of the input number.
3. Output: Print whether the number is odd or even based on the result of the bitwise operation.

## Code

Here's how you can implement this in Java:

```
import java.util.Scanner;

public class OddEvenChecker {
    public static void main(String[] args) {
        // Create a scanner object for input
        Scanner scanner = new Scanner(System.in);

        // Prompt user for input
        System.out.print("Enter an integer: ");
        int number = scanner.nextInt();

        // Use bitwise AND to check if the number is odd or even
        if ((number & 1) == 0) {
            System.out.println(number + " is even.");
        } else {
            System.out.println(number + " is odd.");
        }

        // Close the scanner
        scanner.close();
    }
}
```

## Significance

Using the bitwise AND operator for checking odd and even numbers offer efficiency and simplicity

# Revision

## Key Concepts in Object-Oriented Programming

1. Classes
2. Objects
3. Abstraction
4. Encapsulation
5. Inheritance
6. Polymorphism

## Benefits of Object-Oriented Programming

1. Modularity and Reusability
2. Code Organization
3. Scalability and Extensibility
4. Code Readability

## Components of C++ Architecture

1. Syntax
2. Compilation Process
3. Memory Management
4. Standard Template Library (STL)
5. Object-Oriented Programming (OOP) Features
6. Standard Library
7. Compiler

## How C++ Architecture Works

1. Development
2. Compilation
3. Linking
4. Execution

## Java Frameworks

Java frameworks offer developers a set of pre-defined functionalities, libraries, and structures to simplify common tasks and promote best practices.

## Elements of Java Frameworks

1. Spring Framework - Spring Framework - https://spring.io/
2. Hibernate - Hibernate - https://hibernate.org/
3. Apache Struts - Apache Struts - https://struts.apache.org/
4. Apache Maven - Apache Maven - https://maven.apache.org/

## Bitwise Operations

bitwise operations directly manipulate bits within a binary representation of numbers. They operate on binary digits (bits) of the operands and perform operations bit by bit.

## Bitwise AND (&)

The bitwise AND operator compares each bit of its operands. If both bits are 1, the resulting bit is set to 1. Otherwise, it is set to 0.

Truth Table:

| A | B | A & B |
|---|---|---|
| 0 | 0 | 0 |
| 0 | 1 | 0 |
| 1 | 0 | 0 |
| 1 | 1 | 1 |

```
int a = 12; // 1100 in binary
int b = 10; // 1010 in binary
int result = a & b; // 1000 in binary, which is 8 in decimal

System.out.println("Result of a & b: " + result); // Output: 8
```

**2. Bitwise OR (|)**

The bitwise OR operator compares each bit of its operands. If at least one of the bits is 1, the resulting bit is set to 1.

**Truth Table:**

| A | B | A \| B |
|---|---|---|
| 0 | 0 | 0 |
| 0 | 1 | 1 |
| 1 | 0 | 1 |
| 1 | 1 | 1 |

```
int a = 12; // 1100 in binary
int b = 10; // 1010 in binary
int result = a | b; // 1110 in binary, which is 14 in decimal

System.out.println("Result of a | b: " + result); // Output: 14
```

**3. Bitwise XOR (^)**

The bitwise XOR operator compares each bit of its operands. If the bits are different, the resulting bit is set to 1. If they are the same, the resulting bit is set to 0.

Truth Table:

| A | B | A ^ B |
|---|---|---|
| 0 | 0 | 0 |
| 0 | 1 | 1 |
| 1 | 0 | 1 |
| 1 | 1 | 0 |

```
int a = 12; // 1100 in binary
int b = 10; // 1010 in binary
int result = a ^ b; // 0110 in binary, which is 6 in decimal

System.out.println("Result of a ^ b: " + result); // Output: 6
```

## 4. Bitwise NOT (~)

The bitwise NOT operator inverts each bit of its operand. It turns 0s into 1s and 1s into 0s. The bitwise NOT is applied using two's complement representation, which means the result is the negative of the value incremented by one.

```
int a = 12; // 1100 in binary
int result = ~a; // 0011 in binary for 4-bit representation, which is -13 in decimal

System.out.println("Result of ~a: " + result); // Output: -13
```

Section 15

# Data Structures

# Stack vs. Heap Memory

## Introduction

In the world of programming, memory management is a critical aspect that directly impacts the performance and efficiency of an application. Two essential memory areas in a program are the stack and heap memory. Understanding the differences and proper usage of these memory areas is crucial for writing efficient and error-free code. In this article, we will explore stack and heap memory, their characteristics, and their significance in memory management. In Java, JVM designates memory to variables and objects in either stack or heap memory.

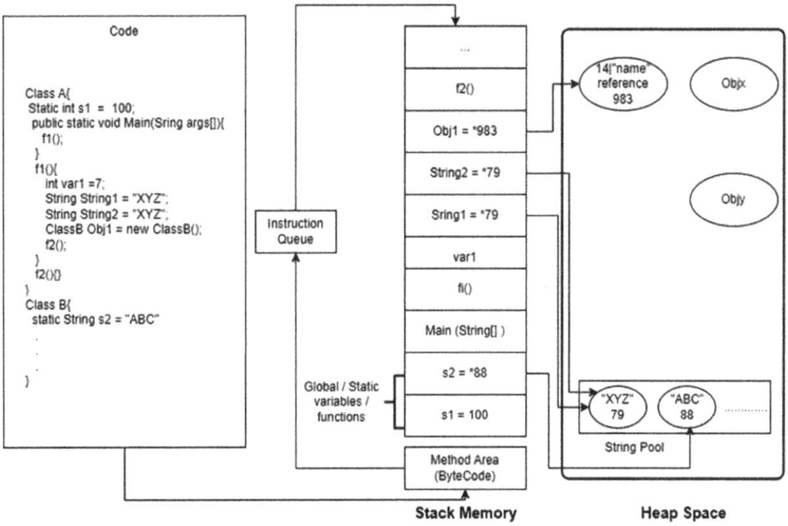

## Stack Memory

The stack memory is a small, fixed-size memory region that is managed by the compiler or runtime environment. It is used to store local variables and function call information during the execution of a program. **Primitive data types** byte, short, int, long, float, double, char and boolean are stored in Stack. Stack memory operates on a Last-In-First-Out (LIFO) principle, meaning the last item added is the first one removed. Once the method finishes, execution, its corresponding stack frame is cleared and the flow goes back to the calling method. If the stack memory gets full, runtime environment will throw Stack Overflow error

Note: Address, i.e. location in heap, of Non primitive data types is also stored in stack. When we assign variable of any non-primitive data type to another variable, it actually assigns the same address. That is why when we change the value through one variable the value in another variable also changes. Memory allocation of String goes 1 level ahead by using string pool. We will discuss that in detail when we will study string.

## Characteristics of Stack Memory

### 1. Speed

Accessing and deallocating memory in the stack is faster than in the heap because of its simple data structure and LIFO management.

### 2. Limited Size

The stack has a limited size, typically smaller than the heap. The size of the stack is determined during program compilation, and exceeding its capacity can lead to a stack overflow.

### 3. Automatic Memory Management

Memory allocation and deallocation in the stack are managed automatically by the compiler or runtime environment.

### 4. Short-Lived Data

Stack memory is best suited for storing short-lived data, such as local variables, function parameters, and return addresses. Variables inside the stack exists only as long as the method that created them is running

### 5. Heap Memory

The heap memory is a larger, more flexible memory region that is allocated dynamically during runtime. It is used to store objects and data structures whose size and lifetime cannot be determined at compile time. If the heap memory gets full, runtime environment will throw out of memory error.

## Characteristics of Heap Memory

### 1. Dynamic Memory Management

Memory allocation and deallocation in the heap are done explicitly by the programmer using functions like "malloc()" and "free()" in languages like C/C++, or through garbage collection in languages like Java.

### 2. Size Flexibility

The heap can dynamically allocate memory to accommodate varying data sizes and structures.

### 3. Longer Lifetime

Heap memory is ideal for storing objects that require a longer lifetime, such as objects in object-oriented programming and data structures that persist beyond a single function call.

### 4. Slower Access

Accessing and deallocating memory in the heap is slower compared to the stack due to its more complex data structure and the need for manual memory management.

## Choosing Between Stack and Heap Memory

The choice between stack and heap memory depends on the requirements of the data and the program's characteristics:

### Use Stack Memory When

1. You need to store short-lived data, such as local variables and function parameters.
2. You want faster memory access and automatic memory management.
3. You have strict memory constraints, as stack memory is limited in size.

### Use Heap Memory When

1. You need to store objects and data structures with an unknown size or longer lifetime.
2. You require dynamic memory allocation and deallocation.
3. You are working with large data structures that would exceed the stack's size limitations.

# Ch 72

# Data Structures

## Introduction

In the world of computer science and software development, data structures play a vital role in organizing and managing data efficiently. A data structure is a specialized format designed to store, retrieve, and manipulate data effectively. Choosing the right data structure is crucial for optimizing algorithms and improving the performance of applications. In this article, we will explore the significance of data structures, their types, and their importance in creating efficient algorithms.

## Understanding Data Structures

Data structures provide a way to organize and store data in a computer's memory, making it easily accessible and manageable. They act as a bridge between abstract data and the algorithms that manipulate it. Each data structure has its own set of operations, which determines how the data can be stored and retrieved.

## Types of Data Structures

There are two primary categories of data structures:

### 1. Linear Data Structures

Linear data structures arrange elements in a linear sequence, where each element has a unique predecessor and successor. Some common linear data structures include:

- Arrays and ArrayLists
- Linked Lists
- Stacks
- Queues

## 2. Non-Linear Data Structures

Non-linear data structures organize elements in a hierarchical manner, where each element can have multiple predecessors and successors. Some common non-linear data structures include:

- Trees
  - Binary Tree
  - Binary Search Tree
- Heap
- HashMap
- HashSet
- Tries
- Graphs

There are some advance data structures like B Tree, B+ Tree etc...

You can design your own data structures as well.

## Importance of Data Structures

Data structures are essential for various reasons:

### Data Organization

Data structures help organize and manage large volumes of data efficiently. They ensure that data is stored in a structured and easily retrievable format, enabling quick data access and manipulation.

## Algorithm Efficiency

The choice of data structure significantly impacts the performance of algorithms. Efficient data structures, when paired with appropriate algorithms, can significantly reduce time and space complexity, leading to faster and more scalable applications.

## Code Reusability

By using established data structures, developers can leverage existing code and libraries, promoting code reusability and saving time on coding repetitive data management tasks.

## Memory Management

Data structures aid in managing memory efficiently. They allow for dynamic memory allocation and deallocation, preventing memory leaks and improving resource utilization.

www.ingramcontent.com/pod-product-compliance
Ingram Content Group UK Ltd.
Pitfield, Milton Keynes, MK11 3LW, UK
UKHW060116010826
14089UKWH00003B/18

9 798894 988283